THE
GARDEN
RESONATES

A GOSPEL
EMERGING GENERATIONS
CAN BELIEVE IN

CHRIS FOLMSBEE

The Garden Resonates:
A Gospel Emerging Generations Can Believe In

Editor: Jack Radcliffe
Designer: Keely Moore

All Web addresses were correct and operational at the time of publication.

ISBN: 9781501844140
PACP10512067-01

17 18 19 20 21 22 23 24 25 26—10 9 8 7 6 5 4 3 2 1

MANUFACTURED IN THE UNITED STATES OF AMERICA

CONTENTS

DEDICATION

For Gina, Megan, Drew, and Luke—

Love you!

INTRODUCTION

I grew up in a garden. It is not even a slight exaggeration to say that while I was a growing child and a maturing teenager, I spent hundreds of hours with my grandfather occupied by working, playing, and quite literally, enjoying the fruits of our labor in his annual garden. It was in the garden, and the countless number of jaunts back and forth to the barn for tools and supplies, that I learned that nothing, including the promise of fruitful results, is given to anyone and especially at no cost.

I loved my time in my grandfather's garden. Mostly, I enjoyed my time in his garden because I was with him—a stern, demanding, and expectant presence, who was able to balance his coarse side, so to speak, with an affectionate, teaching, and empowering smoother side that, in the end, taught me what it meant to work hard and to be satisfied with the work regardless of the outcome. "Some fruits and vegetables just choose not to grow," he'd say frequently. Usually he'd follow that comment up with another that resembled, "Still, if we don't take the time to care for the land and create the right environment, not one of these plants stands a chance."

I learned from my grandfather that faithfulness to the work at hand is imperative to receive the desired results or any results at all, really. The desired results may not always come as we plan, but one thing is certain: Failure to faithfully do the work guarantees that the results we desire won't come at all.

The gospel is like this. The good news is that in Jesus Christ there is salvation and justice, and the church is called to faithfully do the work of God's mission in the world. To witness the world made whole, for people to live into their intended image and for heaven to come to earth, we must faithfully do the hard and difficult Kingdom work that Jesus left the Holy Spirit to guide us to do. Sometimes this faithful work results in the desired results we hope to see in the world, and sometimes it doesn't. The work, however, must be done either way to make our hope an active practice, an enduring way of life.

I felt satisfied when I worked in that garden. It was completely and totally enough for me to go inside for a summer-evening meal knowing that I put in a full day's work and made my grandfather proud. I was also at peace in that garden. My spirit was unrestricted and untethered when I worked in that garden and, for some reason, I think it was mainly my grandfather's presence, no matter what work I was doing—whether I was swinging a pickax or pulling a hoe through the hard-packed mud—I always felt at home or like I was where I was supposed to be.

Even to this day, when I return to visit my grandmother, I can feel myself slip into feelings of comfort, security, contentment, and hope. The garden no longer exists, although some years in the early spring as the grass is greening, you can sometimes see the faint outline of what was once a garden roughly the size of a basketball court. I still feel the peace I felt as a young man when I visit. What may seem very strange to some, at times I can still feel my grandfather's presence.

This book has a very simple premise. The premise is this—the garden of Eden (and the other gardens) was a place of peace—not just the kind of peace that is absent of conflict, but equally important, the kind of peace that comes from being present with God. God longs for the world to be made whole and to be marked by God's loving presence. Parallel to this premise is the fact that humans long to find transcendence that leads to discovering a deep sense of meaning and purpose for their life.

Long before human rebellion led to the disruption of God's notion of peace for the world, there was good—this good is what maintained the peace. The garden of Eden was good or whole long before it was disrupted with evil. Said differently, Eden was complete—it was just the way God intended for it to be. Eden was a place of harmony, of shalom. Therefore, in its completeness, the garden of Eden was unbroken long before it was broken.

People today, particularly emerging generations since that is what this book is ultimately about, long for the very ideas that God originally intended for the world. The Millennials, and their subsequent generation many refer to as Generation Z, are longing for authentic spiritual encounters. They look for these spiritual encounters through meaningful connections with one another[1] and through the desire for a "deep sense of wonder about the universe" and a longing for the feeling of "spiritual peace and well-being."[2] The biblical accounts of the garden of Eden, the garden of Jesus' tomb, and the garden of the new city and the goodness in which God characterized it, resonates profoundly with the emerging generations because of the wonder and peace that is not only reality for some, but a possibility for all.

The emerging generations may not always look to the church and its dogma first to discover and experience spiritual encounters. However, like every generation gone by, emerging generations hunger for a deep and meaningful spiritual life that leads to a purpose-filled life full of possibility. Emerging generations are desperately seeking what can take them outside of the ordinary life and reveal to them the otherworldly life (a countercultural Kingdom way of life) that can generate for them a resounding experience of the supernatural. There is not a better agency on the planet to guide the hungry and thirsty toward the supernatural than the Holy Spirit-empowered-and-driven church. The church, when living out the mandates of Jesus, meaning our faithful pursuit of making disciples, becomes the kind of community where people longing for wonder and peace can find it and participate in it.

The church today, however, struggles to reach and engage Millennials and Generation Z. As a result of this constant struggle, the believability gap between the spiritual voyager and the Christian pilgrim continues to widen. In part, this gap widens for several reasons (we will explore these reasons and their causes throughout this book in greater depth), such as unwillingness or inability to change; a small or lifeless vision; the church's view of culture; the spoken value versus derived value of community; and the apparent disunity among churches, church leaders, and denominations. These and other factors contribute to the widening of the believability gap, and leave churches and church leaders exasperated and the emerging generations disinterested and distant.

---

1. http://www.pbs.org/newshour/bb/millennials-havent-forgotten-spirituality-theyre-just-looking-new-venues/
2. https://news.virginia.edu/content/qa-why-millennials-are-leaving-religion-embracing-spirituality

Deconstruction is easy. It isn't particularly difficult to identify the problems or struggles churches face in reaching emerging generations. Nor is it particularly challenging to identify the behavior and mindsets of emerging generations. What is difficult, however, is constructing a way forward that results in what we all desperately want to accomplish—to reach and engage Millennials and Generation Z.

This book is my attempt to construct a way forward that compels emerging generations, and helps them discover and experience the otherworldly and transcendent nature of a good God who longs to reestablish the Eden peace that showed the world to be whole. Emerging generations will connect with a garden-like way of life and story, as well as the mission to restore the world toward its intended wholeness. Simply said, the garden's gospel story and the mission of God in which it comes from resonate deeply with emerging generations.

I believe that most churches already have the assets and, therefore, the capacity to reach and engage Millennials. In fact, over the last two years, I have worked with dozens of churches and hundreds of church leaders and the end result, in most instances, is that there remains a church that is able to redirect its energies and competencies from desiring to reach the emerging generations to a strategy for doing so.

I think you'll find, at the very least, the remaining pages in this book to be extremely helpful to you as you bear witness to the work of God in the world by being a community of people that invites and ruthlessly welcomes emerging generations into a transformation life of ongoing forgiveness, new life, and experienced conversion toward the image of God.

Myself and so many others I work alongside of each and every day are diligently praying for you as you participate in God's mission to restore the world toward its intended wholeness, like the garden we see in Revelation 22, the garden of the new city that resembles Eden—a paradise restored.[3]

---

3. Henry H. Knight III and F. Douglas Powe, Jr., *Transforming Evangelism: The Wesleyan Way of Sharing Faith* (Discipleship Resources, Nashville, TN. 2006), 17.

CHAPTER 1

THE CORE VALUES AND BEHAVIORS OF EMERGING GENERATIONS

Depending on your perspective, you've either noticed a gradual evolution into what is commonly referred to as a post-Christian world or suddenly the changing landscape of the world has swiftly come upon you and you are just now waking up to the new realities. Either way, as you know, the world is changing and it is changing fast.

It is no longer assumed that the world is guided by the Christian worldview, and that is true for nearly every facet of life—politics, education, sociology, philosophy, and so forth.

In favor of other primary worldviews, such as naturalism or relativism, people have largely moved on, so to speak, from the Christian worldview and opted out of it in favor of a worldview that makes more sense in their minds and in their hearts. In my opinion, this is the most challenging issue facing the church today. Keep in mind, I believe the kingdom of God is never in trouble. However, I also believe that the church is responsible to participate with God to restore the world toward its intended wholeness and, therefore, is both privileged to and expected to faithfully and generously find ways to reach and engage non-Christians.

The new worldviews shaping culture in this post-Christian world, from my observation, typically generate one of two common reactions. First, some people—and I am thinking about church leaders specifically—fear the changes happening in culture and do everything they can to hold on to what they call "traditional values," even at the risk of becoming irrelevant. Often reactors of this persuasion will dig their heels deep into what they know, and usually only what they know and, as a result, often lose touch with the world around them. I speak to and visit dozens of churches that are so committed to the way that church has been or to their "traditional values" and, as a result, they are dying.

A few weeks ago, I was invited to speak to a church near Omaha, Nebraska. The people of this particular church were incredibly friendly and warm to my family and me. For hours we talked about ways that their church might connect with the growing number of young adults and young families with small children in the community. We shared ideas, we prayed together, we ate together, and we strategized together. I was feeling so encouraged by this church's passion to reach the emerging generations, until late in the day on Saturday when, after we had met for nearly five hours, the chairman of the church's leadership board said, "Well, this has been great. You have helped us immensely. I am, and I think I speak for all of us when I say this, ready to do whatever it takes as long as we do not have to change the way do worship."

Oh. My. Gosh. *What did I just hear? Did he really just say that and speak on behalf of the whole church?* I thought to myself. He sure did. To a person, they all agreed that they were willing to do anything, except change, to reach emerging generations. For this group, their way of doing church was more important than their commitment to reach new people in new ways. Needless to say, I left that warm and friendly church feeling like I had taken a punch to the gut.

Second, some church leaders have chosen to adapt and adjust to change, modifying their ministry model within the shifting landscape of culture. In doing so, they have decided to do whatever it takes to understand the culture around them and committed to developing new methods of reaching and engaging emerging generations.

A month or so after meeting with the church I referenced earlier that would do "whatever" it took, except change, I visited a church near St. Louis. I was in town speaking to a group of youth workers, and one of the youth workers asked if I would be willing to stay an extra few hours to meet with some members of their leadership board before driving back to Kansas City. I agreed to stay, so we met for a few hours over dinner and talked about ways that their church could reach and engage Millennials and Generation Z.

The executive pastor spoke at one point and she said, "Chris, we are willing to do whatever it takes. I mean it . . . whatever it takes." With tears streaming down her face, she proceeded to tell me a story about her children who grew up in the church but were no longer actively attending church. She said, "This is not just about my kids. This is also about my kids' friends and their friends' coworkers. This is about every young person in our city who used to go to church or has never gone to church. What do we need to do to get young adults to pursue a life with Jesus?"

I meet some people like that executive pastor who have personal experiences of life in a post-Christian world. Many have raised kids in the church only to have them drop out because many of them see a gap between what we say is important and the way we live. Unfortunately, in most of my conversations with dozens of church leaders like the executive pastor above, the former example of talking change but not really committed to making the necessary changes seems more typical, at least of late. I am hoping to change that, of course.

Most church leaders I know are fearful, choosing to dig further into only what they have come to know that "works" and, because of various forms of fear, are unwilling to explore new ideas and practices that will allow new paradigms of thinking and living to emerge. This reaction has left countless numbers of churches rapidly moving toward a steep decline—both a decline in attendance and a decline in lasting community impact. This means, in the end, choosing to simply "hold on to traditional values" can often result in fewer people being invited into exploring the gospel and experiencing the forgiveness that leads to a transformed life that leads to a world made new.

Several months ago, I was invited to speak at a local businesspersons luncheon on the topic of Millennials in the workplace. I revealed some statistics, research, and some anecdotal-based feelings I had on the subject. The group was deeply engaged throughout my short thirty-minute talk and had as many minutes worth of questions as I did presentation minutes. I spent thirty minutes answering one question after the other, sometimes hearing a question before I could even finish answering the previous question. I love those kinds of interactions!

As I was putting my iPad back in my backpack and clearing my materials from the lectern, I was approached by a man who said, "You are a smart guy, and your presentation was very professional. However, nearly everything you said was just not accurate." I extended my hand and said, "My name is Chris. What is your name?" The gentleman shook my hand firmly and said, "My name is Pastor Mark."

My first thought was, *A pastor at a business luncheon . . . cool!* I asked Pastor Mark, "Why do you feel the content I presented was not accurate?" His response: "Generations are all the same. You don't have to study culture or be an expert on Millennials and Generation Z to know that without Jesus, these young people will die without a Savior and spend eternity in hell."

"Okay, well, I think I know where you are coming from," I said. "First, this presentation was to help business owners and employers understand Millennials. This presentation was not about emerging generations and Jesus as Savior. However, with that said, if we are not students of culture, how do you suppose we will reach and engage emerging generations with the gospel?" I asked. "The same way we always have—by making truth a priority in their lives," he sharply stated very matter of fact. My last question was simply, "What is truth to a Millennial in a post-Christian world, Pastor Mark?" Walking away, Pastor Mark said, "The gospel never changes, and as a minister you should know that."

I agree with Pastor Mark, I think. The gospel never changes in the sense that God's mission to restore the world is always at work in the world, and the gift of God's Son, Jesus Christ, offers unending forgiveness and transformation. However, sadly, the way people like Mark (and the many others like Mark that I meet) think of the gospel and, therefore, build their ministry models around the gospel doesn't often change or transform lives either, for that matter. For many, their approach to the gospel is small—meaning its message is individual, and about a transaction made once with God instead of a community of people learning how to live a transformed life with God. This typically shows itself in the ways some churches and church leaders elect to tell the gospel story—which is having more to do with avoiding hell than experiencing the abundant and new life Jesus came to give us.

This is the tragic reality of our day—churches, who can't seem to get past the way they have always done things to make the necessary and effective change, in order to reach and engage Millennials and Generation Z, stay steadily in decline. These churches remain in decline when it comes to both their attendance (growth) and their community-wide impact.

I never had the chance to ask Mark, but I did sense that, although he had what I would refer to as a very narrow view of the gospel, he did have a sincere desire to help people and see their lives transform. I want to think the best of Mark, I really do. Mark's narrow and small view of the gospel, however, is likely the very matter that keeps himself and his entire church from seeing transformation in the lives of the people in his community, especially emerging generations.

The gospel is very clearly that in Jesus Christ, the Son of God, the Messiah, there is salvation. With salvation comes regeneration, adoption, justification, reconciliation, and of course, redemption. Salvation, and all that comes with it, should bring about a people who live for justice, for the other. Jesus came to form a new kind of people that would, as a result of their trust in him and salvation, live lives marked by compassion and justice. More broadly said, then, the gospel is the story of God's will, way, and work of providing salvation and justice for all of creation through the gift of God's Son, Jesus Christ. This salvation *and* justice, in a very real and practical way, ushers in the kingdom of God, which is already here and at the same time yet to come or be fully realized.

God inaugurated the Kingdom with the incarnation of Jesus Christ and will consummate the Kingdom when all things are made new again and God again dwells with his people. The garden life God intended for this world, as displayed by Jesus, is possible on earth as it is in heaven. This is the hope of the Resurrection—that in the bodily resurrection of a fully dead Jesus, there is opportunity for creation to be made fully alive.

The gospel, then, is in essence God's desire for the world to be made whole (will); the possibility of wholeness through the birth, life, death, resurrection, and ascension of Jesus (way); and the church's responsibility to submit to the Holy Spirit as it seeks to participate with God to restore the world toward its intended wholeness (work). The result of the gospel proclaimed, performed, and made present through words, deeds, and humble company with others points toward a robust Kingdom in which Jesus is the King and in which Jesus reigns in our hearts (spiritual) and in our world (physical).

Mark (from the story above) is accurate—the gospel doesn't change—insomuch as God's mission endures. However, how we communicate the gospel must constantly change in order for us to reach and engage emerging generations. We will talk more about this in a later chapter, but for now let me say that in a post-Christian, post-rationalistic world, we cannot simply present the gospel as a transaction between humankind and God. We must present the gospel as much bigger—as having to do with God, self, others, and the entire cosmos. This is why it is imperative that church leaders take the time to study Millennials and the subsequent generation we call Generation Z, and of course, any other future generations.

The church, at the same time it studies emerging generations, must also be careful not to make quick and thoughtless assumptions about culture. Instead, church leaders ought to become cultural liturgists who can understand and speak the language of the day and find creative and compelling ways to tell God's great good news that in Jesus Christ there is salvation and justice. This, in the end, is the work of a liturgist. To faithfully create moments of worship, we people return God's love back to God and bring glory to God.

THE MILLENNIAL WAY OF LIFE[4]

I am the president of an organization called Burlap. Burlap exists to help churches reach and engage Millennials and Generation Z. We help churches by creating resources, leading workshops and training, by providing ongoing research, and through consulting. For the past two years, I have talked with hundreds of church leaders who tell me that their church struggles to connect with Millennials. For many churches, this struggle points to a bleak future of continued decline resulting in a picture of death. I have literally sat in boardrooms where lead pastors and board members have vehemently thrown up their hands and said, "We have no idea what to do to reach Millennials. We've tried absolutely everything."

Whenever anyone tells you they have tried "everything," do not believe them. Most often this means they have sat around, with good hearts and with great intentions, and merely talked about what they *should* do to reach Millennials.

Often these ideas are met with one or more of the following choices. First, carry on business as usual and pretend as if nothing is wrong and make the most of the life as a church they have left. Second, determine a pathway toward a more vibrant future that reaches and engages

4. http://barkley.s3.amazonaws.com/barkleyus/AmericanMillennials.pdf

Millennials (and Generation Z), and yet choose to do nothing because the work is too difficult and it will mean that too much will have to change. Finally, a third common choice I often observe is church leaders creating more divergence and a wider gap of generations simply by emitting (both verbally and in their body language) the typical stereotypes that Millennials are lazy, shallow, narcissistic, entitled, cynical, restless, lack respect for authority, are perpetually taking selfies, and are only willing to commit to what benefits them personally. Nothing could be further from the truth, in my experience, except maybe for the bit on taking selfies.

As a church leader, don't say you've tried "everything" if you haven't. And please, for the love of God, don't sit there and deny that there is a problem or worse yet, build a case that Millennials are the problem. News flash: Millennials are not nor ever will be the problem and the reason why you can't reach and engage them. The problem is, most likely, that you as a church are exhibiting a narrow, unimaginative, small gospel that compels no one outside the church and barely those inside the church to listen. I am often asked, "How can we reach Millennials?" My response is typically, "The same way you reach any person from any generation or mindset—with a robust, all-inclusive, compelling, embodied, shared, mysterious narrative of the gospel story that points to possibility and away from pessimism and what is broken." The gospel is about a community of people living on mission for the sake of the world. This means that if God's mission is to restore the world toward its intended wholeness, then our gospel message must be bigger than "dying and going to hell." Our gospel, in order to be robust enough to capture the imagination of emerging generations, must be about the possibility of a world made whole, not the probability of a world remaining broken.

Millennials are the largest generation in the West. There are approximately eighty million Millennials in the US alone. In March of 2016, Millennials, those ages 18–34 or those born between 1983–2000, surpassed baby boomers and became America's largest generation.[5] Millennials are diverse too. Roughly 56% of the Millennials in the US are white[6] and by the year 2020, minorities will be the majority in the US.[7]

Following are some other relevant facts about Millennials that church leaders should know:

• The average Millennial has $45,000 in debt.[8]

5. http://www.pewresearch.org/fact-tank/2016/04/25/millennials-overtake-baby-boomers/
6. https://www.brookings.edu/blog/the-avenue/2016/06/28/diversity-defines-the-millennial-generation/
7. https://www.census.gov/content/dam/Census/library/publications/2015/demo/p25-1143.pdf
8. https://www.forbes.com/sites/jmaureenhenderson/2012/03/20/fear-and-loathing-big-retails-beef-with-the-millennial-generation/#6fd230167e03

- Six in ten Millennials have jobs.[9]

- The median Millennial salary is roughly $40,000.[10]

- Just over 80% have donated money, goods, or services.[11]

- 61% percent of Millennials are worried about the state of the world and feel personally responsible to make a difference.[12]

- 84% say that helping to make a positive difference in the world is more important than professional recognition.[13]

- 75% see themselves as authentic and are not willing to compromise their family and personal values.[14]

- More tolerant of races and groups than previous generations (47% vs. 19%), with 45% agreeing with favored treatment to improve the position of minorities.[15]

- 41% satisfied with the way things are going in the country.[16]

- 46% count on social media when buying online, but 55% of Millennials share bad experiences.[17]

You can spend a straight week researching and digesting facts about Millennials and still be barely scratching the surface. My aim in this book is not to throw a bunch of stats at you. You can search those on your own. Rather, my aim in this book is to help you understand the way in which Millennials live. My hope is that you can see how your church can present a gospel narrative that captures the imagination of Millennials so that we might live into the possibility of a world made whole on earth as it is in heaven.

My primary goal with this book is to help all of us who love the church and love people to share a gospel that resonates. I believe the gardens (particularly three of them that I will address in the forthcoming pages in this book) in the Bible and the attributes of God found among them lead Millennials (and all generations, really) toward a gospel worth believing in and ordering their life around.

9. http://www.washingtonexaminer.com/harvard-just-6-in-10-millennials-have-jobs-half-are-part-time/article/2520719
10. http://millennialbranding.com/case-studies/payscale-com-study/
11. http://www.marketingcharts.com/uncategorized/gen-y-engages-in-social-change-19352/
12. http://www.huffingtonpost.com/trevor-neilson/philanthrop-and-millennia_b_3269238.html
13. http://www.huffingtonpost.com/trevor-neilson/philanthrop-and-millennia_b_3269238.html
http://www.bentley.edu/centers/center-for-women-and-business/millennial-research
14. http://www.bentley.edu/centers/center-for-women-and-business/millennial-research
15. https://bornagainminimalist.com/2016/10/17/the-gaslighting-of-millennials/comment-page-3/
16. http://www.pewsocialtrends.org/2010/02/24/millennials-confident-connected-open-to-change
17. http://www.prweb.com/releases/2013/5/prweb10722718.htm

Before we get to the gardens, however, I think it is important to have a grasp on the Millennial way of life. We cannot reach and engage Millennials until we know just who it is we are reaching and the best ways to reach them. If we sold widgets that all looked the same, it would likely be less hard. But we don't sell widgets; we work with people of whom none are the same.

Below are seven core values or behaviors of Millennials. These seven core values come from a combination of Burlap research, Internet searches, and real-time interviews with hundreds of Millennials. This list, it should be noted, is comprehensive but not exhaustive. I've synthesized the research I have done, with the help of so many others, and compiled what I think are the seven main and essentially understood core values of Millennial life.

Seven Millennial core values and behaviors:

1. **Millennials pursue valuable experiences.** A recent study determined that 72% of Millennials would rather spend their money on experiences than on material things.[18] Another study revealed that 52% of consumers purchase experience-related goods over physical items.[19] It is really quite simple—Millennials desire the opportunity to connect with new people and, in doing so, collect shared and lasting memories, particularly with their peers. Travel, food, exercise, co-living, co-working, and so forth, are all examples of areas in life in which Millennials desire experienced-based living. The church can provide experiences, but it must do so in cooperation with the lives of Millennials, not in juxtaposition with it. One of the most experiential ministry initiatives that the church could provide for Millennials is that built around mission work. I would guess that your church could easily adapt the mission work you are doing to more closely align with the lives of Millennials.

2. **Millennials want the world to be a better place and are willing to adjust their life to make it so.** Seventy-four percent of Millennial leaders think they can make a difference in the world.[20] In fact, 32% of Millennials said they are very optimistic about their future, and 40% said they believe they can make a global difference.[21] Just a few years ago, we learned that Millennials have a radical commitment to social change and overall global improvement. We also learned that

18. http://eventbrite-s3.s3.amazonaws.com/marketing/Millennials_Research/Gen_PR_Final.pdf
19. https://www.business.com/articles/experience-over-goods-the-millennial-shift-in-spending/
20. http://nonprofithub.org/volunteer-management/study-finds-millennials-are-ready-to-change-the-world/
21. http://www.care2services.com/care2blog/new-study-shows-millennials-want-to-make-a-global-difference

they routinely pledge to contribute where they are passionate, and are willing to step out and make the world a better place by choosing jobs that are for the betterment of others than self.[22] Again, the church should be leading the way in this, as the interests of Millennials and the truth about the gospel—to make the world a better place, a whole place—clearly overlap.

3. **Millennials are interested in a successful career, but not how previous generations have defined success.** There are six key areas that young adults use to measure success: (1) work-life balance, (2) job satisfaction, (3) salary, (4) achievement of personal goals, (5) achievement at work, and (6) development of new skills. You'll notice that the top two areas, even above salary, are finding jobs that first and foremost provide a work-life balance and provide satisfaction.[23] I needed a new mobile phone a while back, so I went to my provider, and as I waited for the new phone to update and get connected, I had a fantastic conversation with a young adult named Blake. Blake asked me what I did for a living, and I told him I was a vocational minister and also did some other things as well, like consulting. Blake thought it was really cool that I had a job that helped people. I asked Blake why he chose to work at this particular mobile phone provider, and he said, "I used to have a way higher paying job, but I was working like twelve hours a day and I was doing it mostly by myself. This job lets me connect with people all day long. Actually, I love my job because although I don't make as much money as I used to, I get to connect people into relationships all over the world with their phones."

4. **Millennials are optimistic and consistently look for the possibility before the impossibility.** Despite high debt loads, rising global poverty, rising unemployment, less personal income, and so forth, Millennials are quite possibly the most optimistic generation ever (until we look into the Gen Z stats).[24] Innovation and technology have allowed today's young adults to see the silver lining in nearly every situation. The economic bounce back since the 2008 great recession and the ability to leverage technology for one's cause keeps Millennials hopeful. Some say the optimism of Millennials has to do with the way they were raised—confident and believing that can do anything. Others suggest that today's younger generation has a mindset that places them at the center of their lives and in control (think social media) and, as a result, they have belief in themselves for their own future. Regardless,

---

22. http://www.frugalrules.com/millennials-world-better-place/
23. http://www.huffingtonpost.com/brad-harrington/how-millennials-are-redef_b_8710878.html
24. http://www.bentley.edu/impact/articles/nowuknow-unbridled-optimism-millennials

Millennials are optimistic, and the church should leverage this core value and behavior by equaling the level of optimism. Many churches I interact with can only describe what is wrong with the world. Ask them what is right in the world, and you are met with a blank stare. Churches that can reach and engage Millennials are the churches that are correspondingly as optimistic about the future as Millennials are.

5. **Millennials flourish in diverse relationships and environments.**
   Millennials are the most ethnically and racially diverse group of young adults the US has ever seen. A study done nearly a decade ago revealed that approximately 19% are Hispanic, 14% are black, nearly 5% are Asian, just over 3% are a mixed race, and roughly 60% are white.[25] Ten years after this study was published and we've grown in our diversity as a nation, and Millennials have loved it. The importance of diversity for Millennials, however, is bigger than ethnicity and race. Diversity for a Millennial is absolute social inclusiveness. This means that Millennials seek to build a world that is known for its depth and breadth of distinct groups and unique individuals. Millennials have come to expect diversity. It is just plain a part of their everyday life. For your church not to be diverse (think beyond race and ethnicity) and make a way for all people to be included is simply seen as archaic and, in some cases, even considered intentionally exclusive. This does not mean you should manufacture diversity. Rather, you should live in such a way that extends an invitation to all, celebrates different thinking, and embraces perspectives you might even be unfamiliar with.

6. **Millennials expect all parts of their life to be anytime and anywhere.**
   Edwin Hubble changed the way we understood the cosmos forever. His law, aptly named Hubble's law, points to a growing universe and helped us to see that we live in an ever-expanding universe. The iPhone is like this for Millennials. Millennials only know an anytime-and-anywhere world, where nearly all information known to humans is only a few clicks away. This means that Millennials are bound by nothing. Just as the early inventors of the telescope realized there were no boundaries to what they could learn given the new view of the universe, Millennials live unrestricted, portable, and perpetually connected lives that are always expanding. Because of this, churches have the opportunity to reveal the power of God in a way that captures the imagination of young adults and reveals the God of the universe as an awe-inspiring, transcendent Spirit-being that can never fully be

25. http://www.pewresearch.org/2009/12/10/the-millennials/

grasped. Recently I had a conversation with a young woman at our church who said she was just beginning to believe in God. When I asked, "Why are you beginning to believe now?" she said, "I realize that there is no possible way for someone to prove there is or is not a god. This intrigues me. I mean, if we are still learning what is out there in the universe, maybe there is a God. If so, I'd like to find him or her."

7. **Millennials have a digital worldview.** This does not simply mean that Millennials are always on the Internet with their phones in their hands. The fact that Millennials have a digital worldview means that their entire lives are impacted by a digital platform. For example, banking, shopping, exercise, sex, music, work, and so forth all happen by simply reaching into their pocket and taking action. This means that nearly every matter in life is expected to be in real time. Today's young adults expect to be able to connect and engage in meaningful experiences with their family, community, and so forth in any location and through multiple devices. This means that the church must find ways to engage Millennials through intentional communication channels that are native to Millennials. This means that your church may likely need to find ways to tell the story of the gospel in new forms that you've never had access to use before.

THE GENERATION Z WAY OF LIFE

Chasing Millennials is a generation many refer to as Generation Z. Some refer to Generation Z as the post-Millennials, the anti-Millennials, the iGeneration, Plurals, and even the Pivot generation. It is too early to know what name will stick with this exciting new generation. For now, I am choosing to call those born approximately between 2000 and 2014 *Generation Z*. (Depending on whom you read, these dates can range widely, by the way.)

Generation Z is the most educated generation ever. They are more connected than any other generation, and they thrive on all things visual—images and video—to not only entertain them, but to educate them as well. Generation Z values openness, transparency, financial conservatism, hard work, proof, evolving identities, and social justice, particularly human rights, in ways that previous generations did not. The overall population of Gen Z will undoubtedly have a massive impact on the world around all of us as they emerge into adulthood.

Raised in a world that seems much smaller and more interconnected than the world that Gen Xers and even Millennials grew up in, they can be difficult to reach and engage, especially for organizations like churches that are largely seen as institutions in the way of their generations' freedom to form. The wide-ranging reach and expansion of the Internet and the increase in accessibility of information it brings has created a generation unlike any that has come before it.

If churches and social organizations are going to thrive in a future dominated by this massively influential demographic, they'll need to understand what drives this younger generation, what created their cultural ideals and standards, and how to effectively reach and engage them. Unlike previous generations, Gen Z tends to defy generalizations and embrace the idea of individuality and uniqueness as a value and asset, not an issue to be fixed. Many of them have been growing up in families that may include only one parent, two parents of the same sex, three or more adults in one household, or other nontraditional family situations.

Below are some additional statistics from various websites that help us know more about Generation Z in order that we might make some thoughtful insights:

• Generation Z receives $16.90 per week in allowance or $44 billion a year total.[26]

• 58% of Generation Z is either somewhat or very worried about the future.[27]

• 77% believe they will need to work harder compared to those in past generations to have a satisfying and fulfilling professional life.[28]

• 77% of Generation Z is either extremely or very interested in volunteering to gain work experience.[29]

• 26% of Generation Z is currently volunteering.[30]

• 76% of Generation Z is concerned about man's impact on the planet.[31]

Following are seven core values of Generation Z. These seven core values come from a combination of Burlap research, Internet searches and the research aggregated from others, and real-time interviews with dozens

26. http://reports.mintel.com/sinatra/oxygen/list/id=637813&type=RCItem?__cc=1#0_1___page_RCItem=0
27. https://www.jwtintelligence.com/2015/05/meet-generation-z/
28. http://officeteam.rhi.mediaroom.com/index.php?s=247&item=1746
29. http://millennialbranding.com/2014/high-school-careers-study/
30. http://time.com/6693/coming-soon-to-your-office-gen-z/
31. https://www.jwtintelligence.com/2015/05/meet-generation-z/

of today's teens. This list, like the list previously regarding Millennials, is comprehensive but not exhaustive.

I've synthesized the research I have done, with the help of so many others, and compiled what I think are the seven main or key core values of Generation Z life.

Seven core values and behaviors of Generation Z:

1. **Generation Z hates the idea of perfection.** In the hearts and minds of this generational mindset, reality wins over perfection every time. This generation insists that people were born to be real, not perfect. Gen Z does not typically respond to the notion of ultimate beauty or an image of faultlessness or flawlessness.[32] This is good news for the church, actually. The church, after all, is a place of grace, forgiveness, and second chances. This does not mean that this generation doesn't want to be held to a high moral standard or that it doesn't value goodness; it simply means that this generation wants to be authentic in their attempt to create a good world. Sixty-three percent of Gen Z would prefer to see real people in ads than celebrities, as it portrays a realistic world.[33]

2. **Generation Z is not afraid to earn their way.** While this generation is least likely to live for the "American dream," it does have ambitions to be in the top 1%. This generation is ready, willing, and able to earn whatever it is they are awarded. Many believe this has to do with seeing their older siblings awarded for mere participation. Unlike their older and more enabled siblings, this generation seeks to build a pathway for success that is rooted in their efforts and accomplishments, rather than the possibility of being randomly selected or noticed. While this ambition, which looks a lot like the ambition seen among Boomers, can be dangerous as it can lead to an unhealthy concentrated focus on success, it can also be helpful for the church in the days ahead. If the church can reach and engage them, Gen Z will give it all they have to make it "work" or to see whatever it is they are doing as effective.

3. **Generation Z cares about the world, especially human rights.** As our world becomes more and more diverse, Gen Z becomes more and more committed to human rights. If the environment was the primary social concern among Millennials, the rights of people is the primary concern with Gen Z. When we speak of Gen Z being diverse,

32. http://www.millennialmarketing.com/research-paper/getting-to-know-gen-z/
33. http://www.millennialmarketing.com/research-paper/getting-to-know-gen-z/

we need to understand this as not just multicultural but blended. This blended makeup of Gen Z's world has created a deep concern for and a profound commitment to equal rights for all. If your church, or any church, has a robust understanding of the gospel and, therefore, chooses to make this social concern important as it relates to God's mission to restore the world toward its intended wholeness, it will have a great chance of reaching and engaging this generation. To Gen Z, and to the gospel, universal human rights are nonnegotiable.[34] We may not all share the same definition or even commitment to universal human rights, but we must all come to the place of realizing that basic human rights such as clean water and sanitation—and more complicated issues such as gender equality and LGBTQ rights—are a high priority for Gen Z. This means the church must talk about these issues and communicate their plans to help make the world a better place for all.

4. **Generation Z demands evidence to back up claims.** Gen Z, not unlike the others that have come before it, have a "practice what you preach" mentality. We all hate hypocrisy . . . yet we are all hypocrites. Funny how that works. Because of their passion for human rights, Gen Z believes that brands should take a stand on issues, and when brands do, Gen Z supports the brand. Middle ground of the gray areas in life is shrinking. This generation wants things to be black and white. This, too, is good news for the church. After all, we call people to live out what they say they believe. The whole point of Christianity is Christ living in us and doing what Jesus did, not simply walking around saying what Jesus said.

5. **Generation Z is strategic when it comes to their social media participation.** You can understand why a generation so ambitious and intentional about their aspirations would use their social media platforms with purpose. I recently finished up leading an eighth-grade confirmation group comprised of fourteen boys. One Sunday I asked some of them, "What one thing that adults do drives you crazy the most?" One of the boys (the one who seldom spoke any other time) blurted out, "When all they think we use our phones for is video games and sending naked pictures!" Gen Z hates to be viewed as handheld-device mongers whose only purpose is to entertain them. Several days ago, I said to my son, "Can you just put that phone down for one minute?" His response, "Dad, you asked me to find something to read. I am reading about ISIS and President Trump." Facebook, Twitter,

Instagram, Snapchat—they all have their purpose with Gen Z. They choose to talk with friends through one particular platform, build memories via pics with another platform, keep up on world news with yet another platform, and connect with parents and family through others. This, too, is good news for the church. Find out what platform Gen Z is using to interact with your church, and stick to that platform.[35]

6. Generation Z values inclusiveness and the freedom to evolve with their personal identity. One of the most challenging aspects of reaching and engaging Gen Z is our understanding of identity formation. For many of us, we determined our identity early in life—jock, gearhead, nerd, thespian, artist, and so forth, and we stuck with it even to this day and, sometimes, even to the detriment of our happiness. Gen Z doesn't possess an "I found my identity" frame of mind. Instead, for Gen Z, their identity formation, many believe, is not about a one-time revelation but a curated composition.[36] A recent study indicated that "Whether through their Instagram feed or by their gender expression, teens have the ability to decide who they want to be at any given point in time and how they want to share that image. All it takes to change their outward identity is a simple swipe and an upload to Instagram."[37] The many aspects of their lives, especially their social media personas, are melded together to give them an "identity for now" mindset that can evolve as they feel the freedom and consent to make their identity matchless. The church will have to be patient and accepting when it comes to matters connected to the various expressions (think gender, vocation, fashion) of Gen Z. As one young teenager said to me recently, "I don't want to be tolerated; I want to be loved."

7. Generation Z believes the way toward social stability is in the extremes. As we watch Gen Z mature, I believe, as so many others do, that Gen Z will move toward making the world a better place through choosing to identify in the extreme areas of life. The research indicates that personal behaviors will become more conservative and overall societal values more liberal. Along with that, traditional values will become customary as radical issues become more rigid and drastic. Gen Z lives in the extremes and believes that it is in the extremes that walls can be broken down and a better world can be created. The church, unique to its doctrine, leadership, and context, will have to be clear and concise in its articulation of what it stands for and believes in.

35. http://www.millennialmarketing.com/research-paper/getting-to-know-gen-z/
36. http://www.millennialmarketing.com/research-paper/getting-to-know-gen-z/
37. http://www.millennialmarketing.com/wp-content/uploads/2016/12/FutureCast_The-Pivotal-Generation-7.pdf

As inclusivity continues to become a higher and higher value for Gen Z, so, too, will the ambition rise to meet the barriers in our culture.

You'll notice if you look under the surface of the seven values of both Millennials and Gen Z, even in the unique differences between them, there are three common core values that exist and, ultimately, form the overarching structure for life. These three core values are (1) purpose and meaning, (2) common good, and (3) possibility and adventure.

Each of these three core values, more than any other in my opinion, provides the enduring framework for how emerging generations make decisions regarding the gospel, faith, and the church. Let's turn our attention to these three core values as we seek to better understand Millennials and Generation Z in order to reach and engage them through the local church for the mission of God.

PURPOSE AND MEANING

Every person I have ever come in contact with through the various aspects of my life—sports, education, ministry, business, military—has a strong desire to discover their purpose and meaning in life. Sometimes purpose and meaning are used synonymously, and they really shouldn't be. Discovering your purpose is learning your reason for being—the "why" that constitutes our role on this planet. Meaning is the values that you choose to surround your reason for being.

It took me a while, but I have found my purpose in life. My purpose is to surrender my life or my will to God, and to be a conduit for God to make "earth look like heaven" and to participate in God's mission in every way and every day possible. The meaning that forms this purpose or the values that I ascribe to my purpose are the Kingdom ethics that Jesus modeled through his life.

This purpose is where we feel most at home with ourselves—where we live fulfilled, content, and gratified with our life. Most often our purpose is bigger than we are—it is something that we likely never fully realize, but spend our entire lives working toward.

The gospel is like this—it is bigger than any one of us, or all of us really, and it provides a reason for being and the values that shape our reason for being. This is why I believe that the emerging generations are more than interested in the gospel and a life of faith and practice. So many people are looking to make a difference in this world, and the robust story of God's will, way, and work of providing salvation and justice for all of humanity through the gift of God's Son, Jesus Christ, is a very compelling way to make a difference in this world. Whether it is at work, in the home, in the neighborhood, or at the local market, when we live into the gospel in authentic and practical ways, we make the world a better place.

COMMON GOOD

I used the term *common good* in a workshop recently, and I was met with furrowed brows, scowls, and tilted heads. What is meant by the term *common good* is really simple. Common good is simply meant to describe what every person in any given community should share in order to benefit the entire community. Essentially if person *A* is cared for and person *B* is cared for, then persons *C* and *D* should also be cared for. This means that in spite of our differences, each one of us should work for and stand up for the other.

Discovering the other, of course, is what Christianity and the gospel story are all about. We are called to love God and love others, and the way we do that is to love ourselves enough to love God through our ongoing actions of loving others. This, of course, is the mandate Jesus gives us in John 13, to love one another.

In Luke 4, Jesus tells us that he came to preach the good news to the poor, the oppressed, the marginalized, and the prisoners. I believe (and I realize that this isn't always politically correct) that Jesus came for the common good of all because that is what the good news is. Issues such as civil rights, affirmative action, welfare as understood in their best and most authentic intentions, are meant for the common good of all, despite one's racial, economic, educational, and cultural backstory. Many pastors and leaders I know struggle with this concept, but the fact of the matter is that the gospel is like a coin, in that it has two sides. One side is the evangelical gospel, and the other is the social gospel. A robust gospel demands that we not only think about the condition of another's soul and their eternal destiny, but their physical life and present reality as well.

Common good—or the philosophy that all should be equally cared for—does not frame the gospel. The gospel frames common good. A gospel story that does not articulate how a world isn't made better both evangelically and socially is not a gospel at all. This narrow or partial gospel story is just that to emerging generations—partial. In order to capture the imagination of emerging generations with a gospel that they can believe in, the church needs to proclaim, perform, and make present the reality that in Jesus Christ's death, burial, and resurrection there is life—new life for all.

It is important to note that we do not all have to have the same political views to work toward the common good. In fact, that in part is what the common good is—collaborative and bipartisan work to make the entire world a better place. We shouldn't prioritize red states or blue states. Instead, we should prioritize a peaceful state in which all of God's creation is stewarded faithfully.

POSSIBILITY AND ADVENTURE

The gospel is all about possibility and adventure, and emerging generations are passionately interested in both. Millennials and Generation Z believe that the world can be made whole. They may not use that exact language, but based on the research, Millennials and Generation Z long to personally make the world a better place. Millennials and Generation Z ooze optimism. They believe in possibility—that it is quite literally not only probable but plausible that what we all long for can be made real.

The gospel demands that we have hope or, as emerging generations might describe it, possibility. I've never met a person who wasn't interested in a fruitful future. I have met many pessimists who want a fruitful future, but do not think it is attainable. But even each of them desires a future that is marked by prosperity.

The gospel is possible, but it is also a massive undertaking. The gospel demands that we embrace adventure. Christians are pilgrims in the sense that we are on a journey toward wholeness, the sacred ending. This means that moments of excitement, risk, and danger are par for the course, so to speak. Emerging generations are up for an adventure. They, as we have seen from the insights above, are willing to work hard and love to work together, valuing experiences as much as the end result.

Take a quick look at the illustration below. When the gospel is articulated with overarching ideals such as purpose and meaning, the common good, and possibility and adventure, it has more than a good chance of reaching and engaging emerging generations. The gospel, in the minds and hearts of Millennials and Generation Z, is at its best when these three ideals overlap and make significant participation and contribution available.

The gospel begins, not in Genesis 3 with the rebellious fall of humanity, but in Genesis 1 with the creation of all that was called good. The garden gospel, when demonstrated to emerging generations in faithful, generous, and winsome ways, resonates deeply with all those who desire to find purpose and meaning for their life, those want to actualize a common good for all, and anyone willing to see life as a missional adventure.

This is why I believe there is no reason that churches today can't reach and engage emerging generations. The gospel story is already pregnant with possibility and robust enough to capture the imaginations of young adults—if only we'd make the garden-like gospel echo in all that we say and do. This is why I love the church. The church is the agency that God has set apart and called to participate in God's mission to restore the world toward its intended wholeness.

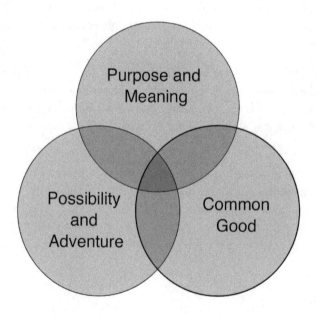

CHAPTER 2

A DEEPER LOOK AT THE GREAT GOOD NEWS OF SALVATION AND JUSTICE AND THE KINGDOM OF GOD

When we attempt to define and describe a word like "gospel," we take a chance. It is risky because often in our passionate commitment to communicate what the gospel is and what it means, we can sometimes focus solely on how our minds have come to perceive it in the midst of a Western way of thinking. This misstep can lead toward a more anthropocentric understanding of the gospel and lead us away from a more accurate biblical context in which we ought to comprehend and define the gospel, therefore, creating uncertainty about what it really is.

Very simply, the gospel is God's will, way, and work of providing wholeness (salvation and justice) for all of humanity through the gift of God's Son, Jesus Christ. In Jesus Christ, there is salvation because in Jesus Christ, the Messiah, the kingdom of God is near or at hand. Jesus' message straight from his own mouth, very early in the Synoptic Gospels, was and is very clear that the time had come and the kingdom of God was upon the people. Therefore, the people were called to repent and believe the good news.

We must take the time (if only for the sake of the emerging generations) to come to a mutual understanding of two terms. First, we must get clear on what we mean when we say "gospel." Second, we must get clear on what we mean when we say the "kingdom of God."

WHAT IS THE GOSPEL?

The gospel is more than Jesus died for us—much more, actually. Yes, in Jesus' crucifixion, death, burial, resurrection, and ascension, there is the gift of salvation and justice. However, long before Jesus' death, there was a life.

Jesus not only came to die for us, Jesus came to show us how to live. Jesus is the way, the truth, and the life (John 14:6). This means that in Jesus, we find the personal pathway to God (way), the exact representation of God and the explicit knowledge of God (truth), and the source and sustainable provision of our true existence (life).

The gospel, therefore, is the good news or message that the kingdom of God is inaugurated in the incarnation of Jesus. The invitation to belong to the Kingdom is for all of humanity, and it is simple—repent and believe the good news. When we choose to believe, we put our faith or trust in Jesus that he is who he says he is, both our Savior and Lord. Jesus is our Savior because he rescues and redeems us. Jesus is our Lord because he reigns in our hearts, minds, and souls.

There are several key aspects of the gospel that we must pursue and trust in order that we might live gospel-shaped lives and, at the same time, reach and engage others with the great good news.

First of all, we must remember this is God's story, not our story.[38] The gospel story began with God's Creation. We are clearly part of the story, but the story belongs to God.

Second, it is also important to remember that it *is* a story.[38] It's not just a collection of facts, it's a beautiful narrative—made up of many smaller narratives—that ultimately defines and shapes the way we live.

Third, the story as mentioned above is about God's will, which is that the world be whole[38] and God's way of making the world whole again through the life, death, burial, resurrection, and ascension of Jesus. The way of wholeness, therefore, is through the life of Christ. We enter into this life by repenting, believing, and following Jesus; by declaring that Jesus is the King of our lives.

The way God goes about revealing God's will and way is through the work of the Holy Spirit coupled with the work of the church. The Holy

38. Adapted from: http://www.christianitytoday.com/ct/2008/march/13.36.html

Spirit guides the church to be about the work of God in the world. To do the work of God is to humbly and faithfully participate in God's mission to restore the world toward its intended wholeness.

Fourth, the gospel is about salvation *and* justice.[38] It's about deliverance and liberation. Luke 4:14-21, as we have already mentioned in the previous chapter, declares that Jesus came to preach or proclaim the good news to the poor, to the blind, to the captive, and to the oppressed. The gospel, then, *delivers* people; it brings freedom from sin. Freedom from sin allows for a healthy and whole life. A healthy and whole life in the way of Jesus leads to desiring that for others. A community of people living on mission who have been freed from sin, therefore, work to right the wrongs of the world. Righting the wrongs of the world ultimately releases people from the oppressions and injustices of this world. The gospel, when fully lived out by the church, provides both salvation and justice to bring about the wholeness God desires for the world.

Finally, it is important to remember that the gospel, in addition to being God's story, is also God's gift. God is a gracious, holy God who is full of love, and who desires for us to receive the gift and be humbled and grateful, and live in such a way that transforms the world. The gift of God's Son, Jesus, is what the story is all about.

Christopher Wright in his book, *The Mission of God's People,* states it about as clear as I have ever read it when he states, " . . . the bible itself will correct our tendency to reduce the gospel to a solution to our individual sin problem and a swipe card for heaven's door, and replace that reductionist impression with a message that has to do with the cosmic reign of God in Christ that will ultimately eradicate evil from God's universe (and solve our individual sin problem, too, of course)."[39]

The gospel provides at least four meaningful elements for our lives and for the lives of those who have yet to come into contact with the gospel. It's important to know that these four elements, when truly lived out, will transform your life and the life of your community, for the sake of the world.

We are here on this earth for the same reasons Jesus was here on this earth—to carry out God's mission, to seek and save the lost. In our context, there are many people who are lost, who are hurt, who are broken, and who have never been invited into the gospel story in a way

---

39. Christopher Wright, *The Mission of God's People: A Biblical Theology of the Church's Mission* (Zondervan, Grand Rapids, MI. 2010), 31.

that transforms their lives. Jesus has commissioned us to reach these people.

First, the gospel **is a pattern for everyday life**. We no longer live into our old lives. Once we declare that Jesus is King, we live new lives that no longer restrain us from the way we were originally created to live. This new life provides a way for us to understand the gospel in a real and practical way. God is a God of life, and God wants us to live into the new lives we've been given. This new life has already been patterned for us by the life of Christ. Christ lived in such a way that revealed to us the intended ways of God. Love, mercy, compassion, truth-telling, humility, service, and sacrifice marked Jesus' life, and these characteristics form the pattern for our lives.

Second, the gospel **provides freedom**. It frees us from the oppression of sin, of poverty, of slavery, of injustice, of every social structure that holds people down. The fact that there are some people who are so poor they can't eat or that some people live in places where they can't get clean water and many others are tragically dealing with issues of abuse, racism, lack of educational opportunities, and so forth, holds people down as others intentionally push them down. All of these injustices and any others in the world today are to be transformed by the gospel as the gospel transforms us. When we do work to prevent these injustices because of our commitment to the gospel, we live into the new life Jesus modeled and illustrated.

Third, the gospel **provides hope and healing**. The gospel provides a new imagination for people, the opportunity for people to see and experience life differently—a world that is no longer governed by brokenness and sin and pain and confusion, but is governed by the kingdom of God and the power, peace, provision, and presence of God that transcends this world.

Finally, the gospel **provides community**. When lived out the way Jesus intended, the gospel provides a place for people to belong and to be who they are, yet at the same time be transformed through relationships. The gospel provides community for all who seek community.

The gospel provides these four elements because God is zealous about restoring the world to its intended wholeness. Each of us is invited to live into the image of God in which we've been created. That image is a whole and complete life that is full of peace. As you think about the people in your life who don't yet have a relationship with God, think about how your life—enveloped by these four key elements of the gospel—can change the world. When you live into the image of God, you reveal the nature of God to those around you, and that is how the gospel transforms the world for the mission of God.

WHAT IS THE KINGDOM OF GOD?

The central message of Jesus' teaching was the kingdom of God. In fact, after Jesus' resurrection, he spent forty days teaching his disciples about the kingdom of God, which is both spiritual and physical, and which has various attributes.

First and foremost, the kingdom of God is **both a present and a future reality**. The Kingdom lives within us, but it is also a future reality insomuch that the people of God will one day reside with God eternally again.

The kingdom of God is **backwards**. The kingdom of God flips our lives upside down. Many times, it is the opposite of our internal natures, as illustrated by the confusing and often surprising endings to Jesus' many parables. When we live out the virtues of God's kingdom, we do so in ways that do not seem logical, and sometimes it just doesn't make sense.

The kingdom of God is **exclusive in the sense that only believers enter the Kingdom**. God designs and governs the entry points for humanity. *Exclusive* does not mean we don't invite others into it. The point is that the Kingdom is a new society, open to *everyone who has committed to Jesus*. We make the Kingdom inclusive when we invite others into it, but ultimately, only believers reside in the kingdom of God.

The kingdom of God is a **place of celebration**. In the kingdom of God, righteousness, peace, joy, and wholeness reign. The wholeness that God intends for the world is an aspect of the kingdom of God that can be present now and will be certain in the future.

The kingdom of God can be understood by **studying the life of Christ in the gospels**. You will see the kingdom of God in the virtues Jesus lives out in his earthly life and ministry.

The kingdom of God is **sustained by the power of the Holy Spirit**. The Father sent the Son, and the Son sent the Spirit. The Holy Spirit bears witness to the work of the Son, and the Spirit's work in each of our lives is what sustains the rule of God.

In addition to these spiritual characteristics, there are three physical expressions of the kingdom of God to consider.

First, **the whole earth represents the kingdom of God**. God reigns over the entire earth. Where is the kingdom of God? Here on earth. Everywhere. The kingdom of God is anywhere God reigns.

The kingdom of God is **reflected in the church community**. The church is tasked with living in such a way that reveals God and God's kingdom.

Finally, the kingdom of God is physical in that **each one of our physical bodies makes up the Body of believers**. We ought to live in such a way that our bodies consume then reveal the kingdom of God. Included in this is how we care for our bodies, how we treat the earth, how we interact with others, and so forth.

The gospel and the ethics of the Kingdom demand everything; it demands that God rule in our lives; it demands that we declare Jesus as the King. If we are going to truly understand the gospel in such a way that we live it out, then Jesus must be the ruler of this Kingdom we are part of, both in a spiritual sense and in a physical sense.

What does it look like when God's kingdom society is lived out for real? There are some postures we can take to use as evaluative or reflective tools against ourselves as we share God with the world in our everyday lives. Certain aspects of the Kingdom are revealed to the world when we truly live as though Jesus was—and is—the King.

First, are we—the church, the people of God—about **humility**? Do we approach the world with a sense of grace and mercy or do we approach it as though we have it all figured out? Do we approach it as though we still have something to learn? If we're going to be faithful disciples who effectively bring the gospel into the world, we must be people of humility.

Second, we must be people of **holiness**. God's kingdom is a place of holiness, a place where righteousness is real, a place where we are no longer held captive by the sins of this world. So, here and now, as gospel-bearers and Kingdom-dwellers on earth—as those set apart by God—we must live lives that reflect the holiness of God. Holiness is a process or a gradual work in our lives where we convert out of our "old self" into our "new self." People who are on their way toward holiness have a total love for God and others, and this total love results in being set apart from the world in the way we parent, pastor, lead, follow, coach, befriend, and so forth. Holiness becomes a priority when we are willing to do whatever it takes to arrange our lives to build in prayer, Bible reading, accountability, solitude, confession, and other disciplines that help us die to self and live for God's mission.

Sometimes it seems like you and I—and the church as a whole—are really good at telling the world what they need to know, but we're not very good at listening to and learning from those around us about what they know about faith and life. So, third, we must be people of **conversation**—not just people who make assertions and polarizing statements, but people who truly dialogue with one another.

Hospitality is a key piece. How do we treat strangers and those who enter the spaces we "own"? Do people feel warm, welcomed, and wanted? In order to faithfully and effectively bring the gospel to the world, we must be people of hospitality.

We also must be people of **generosity**. We must give our time and money. We must be willing to sit at a table with unbelievers and be generous with our words and encouragement. Every once in a while, I will see a meme or a tweet or a post that says, "Build bigger tables, not higher fences," or something to that effect. Some of your best friends may choose not to believe in God, but that doesn't mean you should forget about or ignore them. Don't pretend they aren't important in your life. Instead, invite them to the table. They are just as important as anybody else in your life, and it will be through your generous spirit that you will be faithful and effective at bringing the gospel into the world.

At the end of the day, to see new people coming into God's kingdom, to see people made believers, to get people to repent, believe, follow, and declare that Jesus is King, we must be **faithful**. Sometimes it's easy just to sit back and assume someone else will share the gospel, but the truth is each one of us has to be faithful in doing that by simply living out the virtues of Jesus, revealing to the world around us what the Kingdom looks like. We'll make mistakes along the way, of course. But we will be measured by our faithfulness, not by numbers. Remember the story from Acts chapter 2: *The Lord added daily to the community.* Why does God do that? God does that because they faithfully live out the kingdom of God and the virtues of Jesus in their world.

Each of us needs to live with a vivid **imagination**. We need to begin to see the potential of the world as God sees it. God sees the world as being whole again one day. If we live in a way that imagines that wholeness and if we let it transform our lives, then other people will begin to see, too, how the world can be different. We must be living images of the kingdom of God.

Finally, it's important to commit to **prayer**. One of the most integral pieces to being a follower of Jesus and representing him well is to practice prayer. We pray not only for our own desires and ourselves, but also for the world. We must develop a true and real compassion for the world by interacting with God through prayer. You're probably familiar with the Lord's Prayer:

Our father, who art in heaven,
hallowed be thy name.
Thy kingdom come,
thy will be done on earth as it is in heaven. . . .

This prayer is just one place where we see Jesus interacting with God on behalf of the world. It is important for us as communities and individuals to develop prayer lives that remind us who we are and who we are not. God is God, and we are not. In so saying, we remind ourselves that the world is lost and in need of a Savior, and we have been commissioned by Jesus to take this message of the gospel into the world. One of the ways we can do that is through our own prayer.

THE GOSPEL AND THE KINGDOM FOR A POST-CHRISTIAN MINDSET[40]

Before Stanley Grenz died, I was able to share a meal with him during a conference in San Diego. I'm deeply indebted to Stan for his many creative works, but also for taking the time to help me rethink and reimagine how the gospel needs to be articulated for a post-Christian mindset. That day, Stan spent more than an hour helping me to see that a

---

40. I tell this story and share these points in a previous book I wrote called, *Story, Signs and Sacred Rhythms.* I chose to tell this story and share these points again because of their relevance and application to the content in this book. I have revised the four points a touch to better connect with the words I use in this book.

relevant gospel for a post-Christian culture must be characterized in four ways:

First, the gospel must be *post-individualistic.* Simply stated: The gospel is best understood and proclaimed in community. This is true because the gospel is communal. It isn't about you or me—it's about us.

Many people in a post-Christian world believe that knowledge is wrought through cognitive frameworks mediated by the communities in which they participate. Grenz says, "With its focus on community, the postmodern *[or post-Christian]* world encourages us to recognize the importance of the community of faith in our evangelistic efforts. Members of the next generation are often unimpressed by our verbal presentations of the gospel."[41] This means it's very important to make sure that our students aren't articulating the gospel only with their mouths, but also with their lives. The best apologetic of the gospel is one's life, not mere words.

A community of people who are living and loving in the ways of Jesus and who recognize the importance of a post-individualistic gospel can help the rising generations have encounters with God. Inviting postmodern students into a community whose first priority is to reveal God through Jesus will draw others to Jesus in the communal embodiment of the gospel in the authentic community they share.

Second, the gospel must be *post-rationalistic.* This means that the elevation of reason found in modernism is irrelevant to a post-Christian world living today. A post-Christian articulation of the gospel no longer focuses on mere propositions as the central tenet of the Christian faith. On the other hand, a post-Christian articulation of the gospel is equally serious about the dynamic dimensions of human experience and the attempts of each person to make the most sense out of life.

Third, a post-Christian articulation of the gospel must be *post-dualistic.* We've talked about this concept in this book already, so I'll be brief here. The gospel cannot separate the soul from the body. Rather, the gospel in a post-Christian context must be about a unified whole that includes the totality of a person. A gospel for emerging generations, as we've already mentioned, cannot solely focus on saving souls. Rather, it must genuinely seek to restore the whole person to a society of God. Finding union with God and true relationship with ourselves and with

---

41. Stanley J. Grenz, *A Primer on Postmodernism* (Eerdmans, Grand Rapids, MI. 1996), 167–174.

others must become a more common call to true conversion of broken images of God to newly designed images of God. This, too, the call to true conversion, is an essential part of the gospel.

Finally, articulating the gospel in a post-Christian world, according to Grenz, must be post-noeticentric. (Yeah, I wasn't sure that was a real word when Grenz spoke it either, but I guess it is.) The word *noeticentric*, as Grenz uses it, means that our gospel must become more than the collection of knowledge. The gospel must serve as the gathering of not only intellectual smarts, but also wisdom that leads to Christian formation. A post-noeticentric gospel doesn't allow for the amassing of propositions alone, but it does push for a spiritually transformed heart. Therefore, knowledge isn't for intellectualism's sake, but for the sake of conforming more to the mission, message, and means of Jesus.

The gospel must be articulated—in words and actions—for it to be relevant to a post-Christian culture. Helping our churches understand this necessity and giving them a narrative to begin to articulate and a lens in which to view the gospel is imperative to a church that's leaning into and living out the goals of God's mission—salvation and justice.

CHAPTER 3

THREE GARDENS AND A PATTERN FOR TRANSCENDENCE

've made several propositions in this book so far. Among them are three primary arguments that help us see what it means to proclaim, perform, and make present the gospel in a way that emerging generations can believe in. The three primary arguments to this point in the book are:

1. Emerging generations have a deep longing for and commitment to (a) finding purpose and meaning for their lives, (b) the common good, and (c) the possibility for a better future. My point is simply that in order for the gospel we declare to resonate with emerging generations, it must connect to these top three cravings of Millennials and Generation Z.

2. The gospel isn't merely about Jesus dying for our sins; it is just as much about Jesus showing us how to live. This way to live is the Kingdom ethic that Jesus teaches his disciples to follow. The kingdom of God is anywhere Jesus reigns—in our lives, in our hearts, in our church, and within our entire cosmos.

3. Since the gospel is first defined as the will of God, this means that the gospel isn't a reactive response to the fall of humans in Genesis 3. Instead, the gospel is a proactive design of God in which God created the world to be whole (Genesis 1 & 2).

My proposal in this chapter is simply this: Since the gospel (marked by God's desire for the world to be whole) begins with the creation of the cosmos and all within it, the garden of Eden is an image of a whole and complete world. God's intention is that we live garden-like lives that re-create the garden experience.

In this chapter, I will focus my ideas around three gardens in the biblical narrative—the garden of Eden, the garden of Jesus' tomb, and the garden of the new city. I will attempt to make the case that in each of the gardens, we discover four essential characteristics that ultimately form a pattern for transcendence which we will discuss later in detail, but for now define simply as what is beyond the limits of an ordinary human experience.

This pattern of transcendence, as proclaimed through a robust gospel and kingdom-of-God framework, is what will capture the imagination of emerging generations. I believe the three gardens mentioned above, and the signs of transcendence that emerges out of them, are the most compelling ways to reach and engage emerging generations. There is no secret sauce or fail-proof way of reaching and engaging; we all know that. There is, however, a scarcely applied way of reaching and engaging Millennials and Generation Z that raises the awareness or points to the ongoing signals of transcendence.

Gardens display life, beauty, abundance, serenity, pleasure, and contentment. It shouldn't surprise us, therefore, that one of the most significant themes that frames the enduring and unfolding redemptive story of God's intention for a whole world is the garden motif.

Gardens and the living elements that compose them, such as the soil, water, trees, and foliage, provide evidence of a life that is carefully cultivated and richly sustained. The lush and fully alive gardens we've experienced in our own personal lives are marked by a sense of harmony that points us toward the way we ought to live—abundantly and contented. Think back to an experience you've had in a garden that was overflowing with this harmony. My guess is that any garden experience you've had, especially the ones you've cultivated, planted, and reaped yourself, has left you feeling alive and satisfied.

A few years ago, I was in England with a group from my church. Our senior pastor, Adam Hamilton, was leading a trip in which we were tracing the life and ministry of John Wesley. We were in London for a few days of the trip and had a few hours each day to enjoy the city's sights and sounds. When I was planning the next day's sightseeing, I noticed on my map app that just a few blocks from our hotel was a park—a large park called Hyde Park. Hyde Park is a 350-acre park filled with bike paths, jogging trails, ponds, and so forth. It is a bit like Central Park in New York City, actually.

Since I have been to London a handful of times and had previously seen many of the sites I had already wanted to see, I decided that I would enjoy the few hours I had off at the park. In the middle of the park was a beautiful garden. I stopped in this garden for a few minutes to catch my breath and enjoy the serenity. After what I thought was a few minutes (that was actually a couple hours), I was feeling re-energized. I was also feeling very content and grateful. I was overcome with a sense of peace. This is what gardens do; they help us to see God's intention for our lives—a life of peace.

THE GARDEN OF EDEN

When you read or hear the phrase, "the garden of Eden," you should think *paradise*. The word *paradise* comes from the Persian word, *pardis*, and essentially means enclosed or walled garden.[42]

When we use the word *paradise* today, we think of a place that is essentially perfect or a place that is ideal. Paradise for me is the coastal shore of the state of Maine, where I can sit for hours and watch the waves crash upon the rocky terrain. We all have a paradise—an idyllic physical place or mental space in which we long to exist, if even for a moment.

The garden of Eden (Genesis 2:9), also known as the garden of God, was God's good creation in which God placed humans—meaning the garden was God's gift to humanity. It was good because it was God's powerful and creative act that expressed God's glory and accomplishment.

The garden was pleasant to the eyes and good for food. Two notable trees that existed in the garden were the tree of life, and the tree of the knowledge of good and evil. We don't know too many explicit details of the garden. We can, however, infer from the Bible and the ongoing motif found throughout the Bible that the garden of Eden could be characterized by the following:

42. Herbert Lockyer, *Illustrated Dictionary of the Bible* (Thomas Nelson, Nashville, TN. 1997), 801.

- God's intended design for the world—the way human life was intended to be lived out—which was in harmony with God, self, others, and the entire world.

- Eden was more than a place. It was a sacred state of the soul or way of life.

- Eden was good. God described the garden as good—meaning God's creation was complete, whole, healthy—just they way God created it to be.

- Eden was sacred—it was a place where God was present and where connection to God was available.

- God designed Eden to be a place for humans to enjoy.

- God gave humans everything they needed to thrive. Eden lacked nothing.

- Eden was a place of decision—to love God or love self.

- God designed Eden for work and conservation. Labor was a way of expressing humans' true self and caring for the environment at the same time.

There are many other inferences that we can make about Eden. However, for the purpose of this book, I believe we've captured the essence of Eden. Eden was God's gift and God's design for the way human life was supposed to live under the reign of God. Created in the image of God, humans were meant to represent God with the whole of their life. Humans had a mission—to represent the loving, holy, and just nature of God, and to work with God to care for all of creation.

THE GARDEN OF JESUS' TOMB

We know Jesus' tomb was in a garden because the evangelist John tells us so two times in his gospel writing. John 19:41 states that, "There was a garden in the place where Jesus was crucified, and in the garden was a new tomb in which no one had ever been laid." John 20:15 allows us to see that when Mary Magdalene was mourning the death of Jesus and the thought of his missing body, she confused Jesus with a gardener. Jesus was buried in a garden.

If you were to visit Israel and visit the garden tomb, you'd find a peaceful place designed for worship and reflection where a tomb is clearly evident. This tomb is thought by many to be the place of Jesus' resurrection. Many people, however, believe that the site is merely an alternative site to the better-known Church of the Holy Sepulchre, which is also believed to be the site of Jesus' resurrection.

While we aren't sure which site was the actual site or even if one of these two were the site at all, a stop at either location is powerful and sacred. I once spent hours at each location with a group from my church. We prayed, worshipped, and celebrated Holy Communion together to remember the Resurrection with many of my close friends and church family. So powerful!

Just as with the garden of Eden, the garden of Jesus' tomb is not explicitly described for us. However, here are some conclusions that we can make from the information we have:

- The garden of Jesus' tomb is meant to help us reflect upon the garden of Eden in which humans rebelled.

- The garden of Jesus' tomb helps us live into the hope that through the resurrection of Jesus, God restores the world.

- Because of the resurrection of Jesus, humans can grow toward their true selves, which is to live into the image of God—people who possess the intellect, emotion, will, and freedom to love God and love others.

- Just like Eden, the tomb of Jesus is marked by the gift of life over the consequence of death.

- Jesus is the second Adam, undoing what Adam and Eve put into motion through their choice to live for self (Romans 5:17) and usurp God's authority.

- The human cravings of plenty, fulfillment, love, and completeness that were key characteristics of Eden can be experienced through the events in the garden of Jesus' tomb.

- The garden of Jesus' tomb lacked nothing, just like Eden. In fact, the garden, because of the Resurrection, provides a new beginning or fresh start. New life is more than just a second chance. A "new" life offers a different meaning and purpose for human existence altogether.

I believe it is worth noting that the previous garden we find Jesus in prior to his resurrection, the garden of Gethsemane, might be described as the exact opposite of the garden of Jesus' tomb. While the garden of Jesus' tomb is robustly filled with life, hope, and peace, Gethsemane was not. Gethsemane was undeniably filled with anguish, betrayal, and violence. This contrast is, in my opinion, meant to help us see the two worlds vacant to humanity. On one hand, we have a world available for humans to choose marked by suffering and evil (Gethsemane), and the other marked by hope, life, and light (garden tomb).

Let me remind you that hope is not wishful thinking. The resurrection of Jesus doesn't allow for private, easy wishes you prepare in your mind before you blow out the candles on your cake. Instead, the resurrection of Jesus produces a public hope that one day all things will be made new and, therefore, gives practical and immediate direction for the way we live our lives as Christians.

Emerging generations need a hope that is beyond a birthday wish. Emerging generations need a hope that excites, guides, and renews— that calls to action. This, in my opinion, is part of the gospel story we most neglect in our proclamation that must be told. New life found only in Jesus Christ is not just a second chance to escape the flames of hell. New life in Jesus Christ is a fresh outlook on life that is built on God's love, expressed through the actions of Jesus Christ, and leads toward a heightening conversion out of despair and into complete trust and love.

Clearly the garden of Jesus' tomb and the garden of Eden are symbolic of God's desire for the world to be made whole. Although the physical appearance and settings of these gardens are different, the symbolism is the same—God longs for God's intended world of wholeness to be realized. We realize God's dream when we choose to believe in Jesus and, because of our trust in Jesus, choose to live out the Kingdom values Jesus taught and demonstrated. This is what emerging generations need—proof that the garden of God resonates with truth.

THE GARDEN OF THE NEW CITY

We have a little more information about what I refer to as the garden of the new city than the other two gardens I've briefly described. The garden of the new city, as you might expect, has several key traits that overtly link it to the two preceding gardens outlined.

While it is really important to have the greater context of the whole of Revelation, and in particular chapter 21, I am going to focus our attention on Revelation 22:1-6 to describe the suppositions we can make from this vivid description of the garden of the new city. Here are some conclusions:

- The garden is described to have a flowing river (like Eden). This river likely symbolizes the presence and ministry of the Holy Spirit, the promise of life everlasting, and the enduring and plentiful life God gifts to God's people.

- Like Eden, the tree of life sits thriving and blossoming in the garden on either side of the river.

- The tree of life bears crops throughout all seasons. Every month the tree bears fruit.

- The fruit the tree of life produces is meant for the healing of the nations.

- The curse (Genesis 3) of pain and death is reversed.

- God (as outlined in chapter 20) dwells with God's people upon God's throne.

- The name of God is written on the forehead of the people, and the people are able to see God's face.

- There is no night—the death, darkness, evil, and brokenness of the world is no longer.

- The light (God's glory) is so bright, there isn't a need for a lamp or even the sun.

- God reigns with God's people as the people rejoice endlessly.

- The kingdom of God is consummated just as God has promised, and all things are made new.

The garden of the new city brings God's creation full circle. God's intended way of life is realized, and the purity and flawlessness that once marked the garden of Eden is finally present again. This is the full gospel story—one day all things will be made new, and those who trust in Jesus will experience the wholeness in which God longs to once again dwell with God's people.

The gospel, as we have defined it in this book, is the story of God's will, way, and work of providing salvation and justice for all of humanity through the gift of God's Son, Jesus Christ. Emerging generations need this gospel! I know you agree. The challenge is, of course, to find winsome, generous, and faithful ways to proclaim the gospel.

The garden life or state of the soul resonates as it springs from Eden to the garden of Jesus' tomb to the garden of the new city. Emerging generations who value (1) purpose and meaning, (2) the common good, and (3) possibility and adventure will connect with a gospel story where their values and God's truth overlap.

A PATTERN FOR TRANSCENDENCE: FOUR KEY FACTORS

When someone experiences something that is transcendent, they experience something that is beyond the limits of an ordinary human experience. Transcendence can also be described as otherworldly, supernatural, unearthly, extrasensory, spiritual, or mystical. Every human being seeks to experience something transcendent. We may not always use that word, but every person seeks to discover something bigger than themselves—something that makes the comprehending seem uncomprehending and the ordinary impossible.

The garden events and experiences we looked at earlier as outlined in the Bible are certainly beyond the ordinary. Creation, the miracle that is the resurrection of Jesus, and the restoration of all things are undoubtedly considered otherworldly. In the next chapter, I will present some experiences in the Bible in which individuals experience moments that can be considered transcendent, based on the four primary factors that comprise a transcendent event or experience I will outline throughout the rest of this chapter.

I believe there are four primary elements or ingredients, if you will allow me to use that word, pertaining specifically to the three garden narratives that we've discussed. These four primary ingredients can supersede the moment we find ourselves in and go beyond the realm of the material or physical world.

The four primary factors of transcendence are (1) power, (2) peace, (3) presence, and (4) provision.

Power is the ability to impact or influence something based on authority and supremacy. The result of God's power is awe.

Being omnipotent, God is the definitive source of power and demonstrates God's authority to act powerfully throughout the Bible in numerous ways and for numerous reasons.

We could make a very long list of the ways in which God exhibits power throughout the Bible. As I write, several situations in which God uses God's authority and might come to mind, such as Creation, the Flood, the Exodus events, the provision of food to the wandering Israelites, the appearances of God in the Old Testament, speaking to and through the prophets, Daniel and friends spared in the furnace, the incarnation of Jesus, the miracles of Jesus, the Resurrection, the conversion of Saul, and the list goes on and on.

God's power results in awe. Wonder and amazement go hand in hand when God reveals God's power. God's power was clearly evident in each of the three gardens. At the time of Creation in the garden of Eden, God creates out of nothing. Simply through an imaginative thought and the spoken word, all that we have come to know as real in this world immediately resulted.

God's power is also unmistakably existent at the time of the resurrection of Jesus Christ. God exercised God's authority and, through the mighty act of raising Jesus from the dead, conquering sin and death once and for all.

Finally, we have the promise of God that at the time of the consummation of the kingdom of God, God will again employ God's strength and the result will be a world fully restored to its intended wholeness—a world with no more mourning, darkness, brokenness, pain, suffering, oppression, or injustice of any kind.

Peace (Shalom) is not simply the absence of conflict; it is completeness, well-being, and harmony. The result of God's peace is wholeness.

Peace can be understood as the perfect condition or the seamless state of individuals and one another in authentic community within the entire cosmos. Unlike the peace in which the world declares, the peace or shalom that comes from God is not the result of a battle or war. Rather, the peace that comes from God is the basis for true community and intimacy with God, self, others, and the world.

Peace in the garden of Eden at the time of Creation is very simply the idea that when God ordered the world out of the chaos, God did so exactly the way God intended to. Prior to the human rebellion in Genesis 3, the order of the universe was union with God, contentedness with self, closeness and affection with one another, and a deep sense of enjoyment or pleasure for all that God had created.

Peace in the garden of Jesus' tomb upon the death, burial, and resurrection of Jesus is evidenced in the truth that through the atonement, there is a new order, and the new order of relationships consists of the possibility for reunion with God, renewed content with self, a profound and lasting Kingdom community, and a renewed gladness for the whole of creation.

The garden of the new city contains God's peace as well. God's peace in this garden is manifested by the final order of all things made new. If the garden of Eden establishes order characterized by wholeness and the garden of Jesus' tomb establishes the new order by the possibility of wholeness again through the atonement of Jesus, then the final order in the garden of the new city establishes for all time an unbreakable unity and completeness we might better just call absolute wholeness.

God's provision for all of humanity is God's breath or Spirit within each of us. The result of God's provision is life.

The Spirit of God is given to all of humanity. The spirit, or breath, connects God to humans. The Spirit of God is the gift of life. The gift of life that God so graciously grants humans is unique to God. God is the source of all life—physical and spiritual. Life is one of the qualities of God that separates God from other gods. As God dynamically lives among us and attentively interacts with us, other gods made of wood, stone, and so forth rest lifeless. God is Jehovah-Jireh, the God who provides, and God's provision of life is God's greatest gift of all.

In the garden of Eden, "The LORD God formed the human from the topsoil of the fertile land and blew life's breath into his nostrils. The human came to life" (Genesis 2:7). Life separates humanity from all inorganic matter and carries with it the capacity for existence in ways such as organization, growth, reproduction, and responsive action and adaptation. Life, meaning the spirit or breath we are given as a gift, demands that we depend on God. The simple and often taken-for-granted rhythm of inhaling and exhaling reminds us to depend on God, the source of life. If you are up for it, stop reading, put this book down, take five deep breaths, and each time you exhale, remind yourself that God is the life-giver.

I am reminded of Ezekiel 37, the valley of dry bones, where the Spirit of God takes Ezekiel in a vision to a place marked by death. God asks Ezekiel, "Human one, can these bones live again?" (37:3). Ezekiel's response is simply, "LORD God, only you know." God commands Ezekiel to breathe into the dead bodies and when he does, the bones, now renewed with skin and ligaments, come alive and stand tall. This is the power of God's gift of life. Breath is life, and the absence of breath ultimately means death.

At the garden of Jesus' tomb, we are given new life. Because we all are given the gift of life in the physical sense and because of the resurrection of Jesus, and by the power of the Holy Spirit and our trust in Jesus, we are awakened to the Spirit and granted an opportunity to live a new life in a spiritual sense. All who believe are given through this new life direction, purpose, hope, and ultimately, a new endpoint in life. This is what it means to be born again.

In the garden of the new city stands the tree of life. This tree represents a perpetual life that is sustained by God's love and faithfulness. The tree of life and the crops of fruit that it produces without pause represent a life without death, a cosmos without sin, and an unending healing of the nations. Humanity as depicted by the endless fruit means that agony gives way to relief, and God's provision of eternal life pardons us from an unrelenting existence in a sinful state, allowing us to once again, as was God's intended design for creation, live into wholeness, harmony, and in complete relational unity with God, self, others, and the entire cosmos.

God's presence with humanity, and within all of creation, reveals God's desire for a close and personal relationship. The result of God's presence is intimacy.

When I think of God's presence, the first verse that comes to mind is John 1:14, "The Word became flesh and made his home among us. We have seen his glory, glory like that of a father's only son, full of grace and truth." I am also reminded of the many references to the temple, the location where God's presence abides, throughout the Bible. God chose throughout the Bible to manifest God's presence locally. That is to say, God descended from God's throne and made God visible in some form or fashion—bright lights, smoke, fire, a dove, and so forth.

I am also quickly reminded of God's presence when I read Exodus 33 and Moses begs for God's presence to go with him and the people because he knows that God's presence is the only thing that separates the nation of Israel from all the other people on the earth. God tells Moses, "My presence will go with you."

God's presence undoubtedly demands fear and trembling, and this is an appropriate response. God's presence also offers comfort, strength, courage, guidance, and so forth in times of suffering, worry, and mourning. God's presence is a blessing. Yes, we should remember that God demands our fear and respect, but we should also remember that God's presence is an experience that should bring joy and contentment. God's presence should also bring us to a place of humility and should direct our behavior to be pleasing to God. We pursue holiness in the Christian life not merely to be people of piety, but to be people who reflect God's glory back toward God.

The Hebrew word for "presence" is *panim,* which can also be translated as "face," which implies a close and personal encounter with God.[43] Think back to your Bible reading and study of Genesis when Jacob and Esau have their reunion in chapter 33. Jacob tells Esau, "Seeing your face is like seeing God's face" (33:10). God's "face" is a symbol of God's immediate and accessible presence.

In the garden of Eden, God's presence is understood in both God's powerful display of God's glory (Let there be light!), as well as God's desire to be near Adam and Eve in the garden (Genesis 3:8). God clearly

43. http://www.biblestudytools.com/dictionaries/bakers-evangelical-dictionary/presence-of-god.html

desires a deep level of intimacy with human beings as God meets with humans face-to-face.

The very fact that God desires offspring and created humans is reason alone to believe that God longs to dwell with God's creation. However, God's descent into where humanity resides displays God's longing to dwell peacefully with God's creation.

In the garden of Jesus' tomb, God is very literally present with humanity when God, the risen Son, reveals himself to Mary Magdalene. Mary confuses Jesus with who she believes is the gardener, until he calls her name and she breaks from her mourning to rejoice in the fact that not only has Jesus' body been found, but he is risen! Upon Jesus' prompting, Mary leaves the garden, races back to the other disciples, and exclaims, "I've seen the Lord" (John 20:18), and she continues to tell the disciples of her experience.

What comfort, joy, and excitement it must have been for Mary to see Jesus' face—to recognize Jesus as her friend, as her Savior. This is what the presence of God does—it produces an unparalleled intimacy that heightens the relational senses of our soul. For Mary to see Jesus' face was not only to realize Jesus was alive, but to also realize Jesus was truly her God. "I'm going up to my Father and your Father, to my God and your God," Jesus said (John 20:17). God longs to be with God's children.

The garden of the new city also reveals God's deep longing for continued intimacy with God's people. Revelation chapters 21 and 22 very clearly speak of God's "dwelling" with God's people. Verse 3 of chapter 21 reads, "Look! God's dwelling is here with humankind. He will dwell with them, and they will be his peoples. God himself will be with them as their God." Equally as clear is chapter 22:4, which reads, "They will see his face, and his name will be on their foreheads." Clearly, God longs to be with God's people.

Before we move on to discuss the application (or the *So what?*) of the pattern for transcendence as seen through the four ingredients of power, peace, provision, and presence specifically as it relates to proclaiming a gospel that emerging generations can believe in, take a glance at the table on the following page. This table is simply meant to provide you with a summary of how the three gardens in the Bible gives us a picture of what God's intended design for the past, present, and future of humanity is.

	GARDEN OF EDEN - the way the world should be	GARDEN OF JESUS' TOMB - the way the world could be	GARDEN OF THE NEW CITY - the way the world will be
GOD'S POWER {AWE}	Creative action	Conquering death	Concluding death
GOD'S PEACE {SHALOM}	Order	New Order	Final Order
GOD'S PROVISION {LIFE}	Life	New Life	Restored Life
GOD'S PRESENCE {INTIMACY}	Face	Name - "Mary"	Name on Forehead/See God's face

WHY DO THE FOUR P'S MATTER?

The gospel has gotten small; we've made it that way. We need to open wide the door of the gospel and allow people, particularly emerging generations since this is what the book is about, to see the gospel as bigger than an individual sin problem. The gospel is a story, yes, but it is a big story and the whole story too. The gospel is not a reaction to the problem of sin. The gospel is the great good news that God created the world to be whole from the beginning. Yes, of course, Jesus' life, death, burial, resurrection, and ascension bring the possibility for a world to be whole again. And the key word is *again*—the world was good before it was bad; it was unbroken before it was broken; it was light before it was dark.

The church must find ways to tell the whole of the gospel story, not merely a portion of it. There is an interested world out there that is clearly spiritual or looking for transcendence, and all that we've been able to give them is a rigid, small, and partial gospel that is neither compelling nor convincing. If you want to reach emerging generations, the gospel must be much bigger than Jesus died for your sins. The gospel must be presented in a way that reveals the garden life—the kingdom of God— which exhibits God's intended way of life. God's intended way of life is simple really. It is not, I might add, you are broken and need to be fixed. Rather, it is that the desire you have for this world is possible. We can achieve, together, a garden-like existence that oozes with the very elements that make a garden compelling—beauty, growth, vibrancy, serenity, fulfillment, and honest labor that is definitely worth the time.

56

Recently I was teaching some of the content from this book at a workshop at a church near Atlanta. At one of the breaks, a pastor approached me and said, "I love this stuff, but it isn't new. I've been teaching a whole-narrative gospel for years." "Right. This, in fact, is very old," I said with a bit of a smirk. I continued by asking him the question, "If you have been teaching this for years, then you must have some awesome stories to share of people who have experienced transformation as a result of your teaching. Would you be able to share some of those stories with our group?" My question was met with a blank stare that must have lasted ten seconds before this pastor responded by saying, "Well (he chuckled a bit and looked at me like I was naive), just because I've been teaching it doesn't mean the people in my church are living it. I mean, there is a difference between teaching it and doing it."

Yes, there is a big difference between teaching something and people applying what you are teaching. The whole point of teaching, however, is to compel and assist people to be able to do what you teach. For instance, I am a baseball coach. I coach twelve-year-olds. Just because I teach them a technique or practice doesn't mean they'll do it. It is my job to translate the concept into performed reality. The whole point of being a follower of Jesus is to actually do what Jesus did.

So many of our churches only talk about the gospel; they don't live it. The good news must be proclaimed, performed, and made humbly present. We must become churches where we create garden-like environments. Our mission, methods, and message must be driven by God's power, peace, provision, and presence. Cultivating these four elements in our churches is half the job, however. The other half is finding ways to create garden-like environments outside of the church where power, peace, provision, and presence are visible, accessible, and tangible. The places we work, live, and play should be places that we are cultivating garden-like lifestyles where transcendence can be experienced. The baseball diamond where I sweat in the Midwest summer heat can be a garden. The office where you work, the health club where you work out, the pub you like to frequent, the seats near your season tickets at the stadium or arena, and even the place where you shop can be a garden-like setting in which people can experience the power, peace, provision, and presence of God.

I don't want to give the impression that the four P's are some kind of formula or prescription where God has promised to show up and wow people. In fact, we are the ones called to live in such a way that piques the interest of spiritual but not religious people. I get why people take issue with organized religion. So much of it is small and uninteresting. The people who have no religious affiliation—called "nones"—or are atheists, agnostics, or who say their religion is "nothing in particular," make up approximately 23% of the US population. Thirty-five percent of Millennials are nones, and that number continues to increase.[44]

From my perspective, there is good reason for this. Religion (which is not a bad thing) and the way churches practice it has become so rigid and small that it leaves people looking to find transcendence via other means. This is why we often refer to people as spiritual but not religious. People of all ages and mindsets, but especially emerging generations, want to experience something beyond the ordinary, but the church can't seem to locate how to provide those experiences.

I believe a garden-like environment can produce transcendent experiences for people. This is why the title of this book is *The Garden Resonates: A Gospel Emerging Generations Can Believe In*. We must, however, find more meaningful ways to cultivate garden-like settings in which the power, peace, provision, and presence of God can be experienced. We cannot, however, only create these experiences in our churches. We must also create these experiences in our daily lives—where we work, live, and play.

I want to conclude this chapter by sharing some practical ideas on how you can create biblical garden-like settings in which to proclaim, perform, and make present the gospel, which can lead toward shared experiences of transcendence. I will discuss specific signs of transcendence and how people experience these in more detail in the next chapter.

PRACTICAL WAYS TO BEGIN CULTIVATING GARDEN-LIKE ENVIRONMENTS WITH EMERGING GENERATIONS:

- **Gather where Millennials and Generation Z are not where you want them to be.** People typically gather around like-minded people—coffee shops, restaurants, pubs, sporting events. You may have to work to find where the emerging generations hang out. When you do discover where it is they hang out, don't be a dork. Don't be that person who tries too hard to fit in . . . just make sure to be present and available. Interact for

---

44. http://www.pewresearch.org/fact-tank/2015/05/13/a-closer-look-at-americas-rapidly-growing-religious-nones/

sure. Don't just sit there and be silent. Feel free to talk to people, just be winsome and socially aware. I know a person from my church who volunteers his time at high-school debate competitions as a judge in order to just be around teens and learn from them.

- **Invite people to enjoy what you enjoy.** I like to play golf. I am not very good at it, but I like to play. Last summer I invited one of my coworkers, who is a Millennial, and asked him to bring two friends. We had a great foursome and had lots of fun.

- **Listen to their story.** Take the time to ask about a person's life and then be willing to listen. One of my favorite questions to ask a person is, "What do you do for fun?" You'd be amazed at the number of people who have shared their whole life story with me as a result of a nonthreatening question about what a person enjoys.

- **Ask questions.** I have a friend who desperately wants to share with emerging generations his life's story. He spent five years in prison and wants to help younger people avoid making a similar, life-altering series of mistakes. He has a powerful story and is incredibly articulate. The problem, however, is he never shuts up, so people don't want to talk with him. Be sure to let people speak about their own lives. Just as you want to "tell your story" to anyone who'll listen, so, too, do others.

- **Celebrate a local win.** A few years ago, the Kansas City Royals won the World Series. After the Royals won it all, we threw a massive party for the community. I met so many new people that day because, well, who doesn't love a good party?!

- **Buy their artwork.** A lot of Millennials and Gen Z express themselves through art—photography, painting, sculpting, and so forth. One of the easiest ways to cultivate a garden-like environment with others is by offering to purchase their art.

- **Hire them to do a job.** I've hired people before for work that I didn't even really need done. I knew they could use some extra income, so I hired them. Then, I worked alongside them for the duration of the job. It helped out the person needing some extra cash, and it helped me to get some yard work done, all the while building a friendship.

- **Get out of your comfort zone, which likely means leave your house.** Sounds simple, but if you want to engage people in the cul-de-sac and in your neighborhood, you'll have to get out of your house. What if the "ends of the earth" Jesus talks about in Acts 1 is the end of the driveway?

- **Meet specific needs in your community.** Participate in the canned food drives, the school supplies drives, and so forth. Don't just participate, however; intentionally ask some others, particularly emerging generations, to help you.

- **Be generous with your time and energy.** Stop looking at your watch. Are you really in that much of a hurry all the time? We all know that taking the time to be present with people and to use our available energies to be with others make a huge impact in the hearts and minds of others.

- **Walk when possible.** Are there places where you can walk to? If so, do it; you'll meet lots of people along the way.

- **Show up, often.** I can be found at a local establishment several times a week. This is not for any reason other than it puts me in touch with people on a regular basis. What used to be a few chairs spread out with people sitting quietly by themselves has become, at my hangout, a group of people circling their chairs to be with one another. That happens over time and because you show up often.

- **Participate in citywide programs or events.** Run, walk, march, community garden, cleanup day, and so forth. What is happening in the city that you can participate in and meet new people? Millennials love experiences, and they look for them to find enjoyment in doing so.

- **Get a part-time job.** I have a friend who is retired. He was bored, so he decided to get a part-time job as a server at a restaurant where he could meet people and get to know their stories. He meets young adults all the time and invites them to our church . . . and they come! This is because over time, he has established trust with people through his part-time job.

- **Share your story.** Your story of conversion is powerful. It is your story, and no one can take it from you. Your story is also portable; it travels with you wherever you go. Your story is personal—it happened to you. Finally, your story is practical; it is real. Don't be afraid to cultivate garden-like environments by sharing your faith story.

CHAPTER 4

TRANSCENDENCE: THE KEY TO REACHING EMERGING GENERATIONS

I have the privilege of speaking to and consulting with dozens of churches throughout the US and in Canada. Sometimes I find myself speaking to large groups of churches that belong to a regional or local network or denomination, and sometimes I can be found in a conference room or boardroom in a more intimate setting with a particular church's leadership team or council. Whatever the setting, I can almost guarantee that I will be asked the question, "So what is the secret to reaching Millennials?" Often the question, when I pry a little deeper, also implicitly includes Generation Z. Most church leaders that I meet with haven't yet discovered that term, and anyone under the age of 35 to them is considered a Millennial.

My response to the question about the secret to reaching Millennials and Generation Z is one word: *transcendence*. I actually believe this is true of not only emerging generations, but every generation we have seen throughout history. Every person I have ever met, regardless of age or mindset, longs to experience an aspect or aspects of life that emerge out of the ordinary and yet surpass or go beyond the ordinary to produce an experience characterized by words like *supernatural, mystical,* or *otherworldly*.

As it pertains to emerging generations and religion, there are two primary categories that drive the way people think about those who are considered, either by themselves or by others, to be spiritual but not religious. To be spiritual but not religious, according to some recent research, means that a person is either (1) spiritual and not interested in faith, or a person is (2) spiritual yet chooses not to believe in God and, therefore, has no faith.[45]

The first question we must wrestle with is not, "Why are people spiritual but not religious?" but instead, "What does it mean to be spiritual?" To be spiritual simply means that a person is aware of and attentive to what is beyond the physical world. Something that is spiritual in nature is nonmaterial or intangible. It is widely understood that something that is spiritual can be felt, but not necessarily seen or touched and, therefore, connects more to the soul and sometimes even the mind than the body.

Think about what is spiritual to you. For some, art experienced through expressions like film, music, and painting is spiritual. One of my friends went to a concert recently. A few days after the concert when I saw him, I asked, "How was the concert the other night?" My friend's response was, "It was great. It was one of the most spiritual experiences I have ever had." When we experience something spiritual, we are usually moved emotionally, and something within our soul is stirred to make us think, feel, and be in a way we rarely or only occasionally experience.

To be spiritual but not religious, therefore, is to desire to experience something that is moving and soul-stirring—outside of the ordinary—but thought of as unable to be experienced through the religious constructs that people have come to suppose exist. For many, religion is merely an institution or an established tradition that does not offer the spiritual, but instead offers the rote, rigid, and rules-based behavioral modification plan. This plan, in the minds of those who are considered spiritual but not religious, is small and more about making the institution stronger instead of making people and the world we live in a better place.

Recently, my wife and I were out for an evening walk in our neighborhood. We came upon one of our friends also out for a walk to enjoy the warm and bright summer sun. After small talk to catch up, I asked, "So how is everything at church? Are you still playing drums in the worship band?" My friend's response was, "I was hoping you weren't going to ask me about church. Actually, I don't go to church anymore. After three years of attending every week and helping out with the music, I realized that the only thing the church I was attending cared about was trying to build up the church's brand. I don't want to go to a church that is about building its brand and doesn't help me experience God."

45. https://www.barna.com/research/meet-spiritual-not-religious/?mc_cid=b5fc45ce32&mc_eid=e77c8a2c8c

People like my friend, and many others I meet, want to experience the transcendence of God—to pursue the unknown, to grapple with the idea of God as incomprehensible and post-rational, and to feel God's presence nearby—by drawing toward God through the emotions and feelings being stirred by something that is outside of the normal, mundane, ordinary life. This is not to say that God is not in the mundane. God is certainly in the everyday routine as much as God is in the rare and remarkable.

People want to feel something. To crave feelings of one kind or another is human. We were created to feel. We want to feel accepted and loved—comfort, pleasure, significance, growth, and so forth. We also at times want to experience the other side of the emotional spectrum and feel angry, sad, and fearful to put us in touch with our humanness. This, contrary to some people's thinking, is not a bad thing. Every one of us wants to feel or sense something special or unique, and yet when it comes to church and our worship services in particular, we avoid helping people feel and, in its place, we push information and intellectual stimulation. We don't, generally speaking, go to a movie or to a show or to an art gallery or to a ball game to just learn more about the game, although that can happen; we go to have our heart stirred in one way or another. We go to these places to connect deeply with our inner life, with our spirituality.

I don't blame emerging generations for being spiritual but not religious. In fact, I find comfort in knowing that young adults and maturing children and teens have a deep sense of spirituality and crave to experience something beyond the norm—something otherworldly. The challenge is this: Can the church adapt away from its current mode of representing God through mere information-shoving and behavioral modification and instead adapt toward a more spiritual experience? Can we make a new culture driven by connection to God, self, and others, instead of institutional advancement?

I realize that as churches, we cannot manufacture transcendent experiences. We cannot order the kit on Amazon or through our local hardware store, open it up, and make it work. However, we can and should move our congregations toward a garden-like way of life that proves to be outside the norm—or beyond the ordinary—and captures the imagination of emerging generations. We can live in such a way that helps the people around us feel something—the love of God.

TWO PREVAILING NARRATIVES OF THE CHURCH IN CULTURE

As I mentioned earlier, I have the opportunity and privilege to meet with dozens of churches each year. Typically our conversations surround the theme of reaching and engaging Millennials and Generation Z. Some churches that I meet with focus their attention on trying to keep those already in the church engaged. Other churches work to develop strategies that reach people not already engaged in church. Regardless of the driving priority, I typically see two prevailing narratives at work among churches desiring to reach and engage emerging generations.

The first narrative I see is the narrative of *relevance*. Churches organize and coordinate their efforts toward one ultimate goal—being viewed as current, or hip, with the times. These churches want to make a lasting impression on and impact in the community, so they do everything they can think of to emanate a narrative that they "get it" or that they are up on the trends, styles, and movements of contemporary times.

From my experience, these churches spend so much time trying to project a "we get it" mentality that they often neglect what it means to be the church—the called-out ones, gathered together to represent the body of Christ (Ephesians 1:22-23) in and for the community and world.

Not long ago, I was asked to help a church think about new ways they might reach a younger segment of their suburban community. I flew into the city, checked in to my hotel, made my way over to the church, and waiting for me in the lobby of the church was the lead pastor, the executive pastor, and the young adult pastor. After small talk, before we even really made our way into the conference room where we would eventually spend the next two days in strategy and planning, the executive pastor proudly said, "As you can see, we've spent a lot of money to make our lobby look and feel like a Starbucks. Our decor has carefully been chosen, and our overall design is meant to make new people feel like we are not even really a church."

This is not the only church that I have met with that has been driven (with the proper intentions and big heart, I might add) to create an environment that is relevant or made to connect with what the church thinks the community wants.

Another church that I met with recently, surrounded by a community of young families with small children, decided to build an indoor play area for the families in the community to use as they desired. It was practical, safe, and looked like a bunch of fun for kids. I asked a simple question: "How many families from the community, not people already in your church, do you think have used it?" The pastor's response was, "I am not sure. It doesn't seem to get much use, really. Our building is only open four hours a day—from 10 a.m. to 2 p.m.—and most of the kids who would use it are in school." Again, in an attempt to be relevant to the community, the church decided to spend tens of thousands of dollars to build an indoor play area that the community couldn't really even conveniently access. Desiring to be driven by relevance can lead churches to make poor decisions.

I am sure you are thinking, *What's wrong with being relevant?* My response is simple: "Nothing, as long as you actually are." Most churches that live according to the relevance narrative are in such a hurry to connect that they don't even ask what the community needs or do the hard work of discovering what would help the community most. Relevance, which is not a bad thing especially when understood as closely connected and appropriate to the needs of the community, is a great driving principle or priority. However, when it is more about creating the notion that you as a church or a leader "get it" and are hip to the times is not helpful in the long run.

Churches that are trying to be relevant without being culturally savvy or contextually appropriate will live in a constant state of frustration. When churches attempt to mirror culture to be relevant, they usually fall short. As one Millennial recently told me, "If the message of the church is the same as the message of culture, I will choose culture every time. The church cannot afford to compete with culture, and if it sounds like a message I can get anywhere else, why and how is it distinctly Christian?"

The second narrative I often see churches prioritizing is what I call *counterculture.* To be countercultural is to be comprised of different ethics, behaviors, and standards than that of mainstream society. The church should be countercultural, yes. As Christians, we are called to a different set of ethics. Churches should be driven, not by the values of the empire so to speak, but of the kingdom of God. This countercultural narrative is precisely the vision and practice of the early church we see in the Book of Acts. Often, however, many people view countercultural as the need to be emphatically right, devout, or the "only" way.

When I was a youth pastor, we carried out a very interesting experiment one night. As the students were making their way from the parking lots into the youth room, we told them that although there were three different hallways they could walk down, the only hallway they could use to get to the youth room was the one that took them down the most maze-like hallway. We positioned leaders at the ends of each hallway that was not accessible that night and funneled everyone down one hallway. The comments of the students were hilarious. We heard everything from, "But I always use this hallway!" to "This is stupid," to "That's the dumbest thing I ever heard," to my favorite which was, "This makes absolutely no sense. You've lost your minds. Who cares how I get there as long as I get there?!"

The point was simple. When we force people out of the normal rhythms of their lives and make them experience something that is outside the norm, it makes people feel awkward, uncertain, confused, and unwelcome. Yes, of course, the church should call people toward God's intended way of life, but the church should do so in generous and winsome ways that don't leave people feeling awkward, uncertain, confused, or worst of all, not welcomed.

Many of the churches I meet with have good intentions. They want to live as Jesus is calling them to live. However, the way they choose to express this desire is more often seen as judgmental, hypercritical, or even exclusive. Unintentionally, we can create environments that are marked by exclusion instead of inclusion, hostility instead of hospitality, and fault instead of faith.

When my wife and I moved from Chicago to Kansas City over a decade ago, we visited a dozen or so churches before we landed on where I currently attend and serve on staff, The United Methodist Church of the Resurrection. It took us weeks to find Resurrection, but when we did, we knew we were at home.

The very first visit, we were met with a message that stirred my soul and moved us to action, literally. My wife and I signed up to serve in the community through several of our church's various initiatives that day. We were called and challenged to participate in the Kingdom work in a countercultural way and accepted that challenge. I vividly remember that the invitation and communication to participate was done in a generous way—a way that honored all people. Newcomers and long-time members were made to feel like contributors to the work instead of feeling guilty or pressured into helping. The sermon that day was undoubtedly anti-empire, but never did it come across as exclusive or judgmental or like the church "had it all together."

Churches are made up of people. People are always in progress. The progress or conversion is to be made into the image in which we were created—the image of God or what is sometimes referred to as fully human. However, in an attempt to call people to conversion, we can alienate people and make them feel as though they are not good enough. The way of Jesus is countercultural but is to be marked by grace, mercy, justice, and hope, not hate, despair, and judgment. You think your church is the former and not the latter? I hope so, but you should ask the people in your community how they feel about your church. Don't ask yourself how you feel about your church. You'll likely lie to yourself and make yourself out to be better than you really are. We do this all the time. It is so hard to tell ourselves the truth; we don't like the pain associated with the truth, so we spin alternative narratives.

Working with a church a while back, we surveyed one hundred people in their community. We asked the people in the community, all nonchurchgoers and friends of those in the church, to describe the church if they had personal experience with it or to comment on their personal perception of the church if they didn't. The results were astounding. Before I give you the results of the community, however, let me give you the results of the church. The people within the church described the church as "friendly," "caring," and "family." The people in the community described the church as "arrogant," "wealthy," and "defensive."

It isn't always the way we think it is. Do the hard work, and ask your community how they feel about your church. It is fine to live by the countercultural narrative, of course. You are a church. You are supposed to hold to different values and set of ethics. The manner in which you do, however, can make all the difference in the world to the eyes, ears, hearts, and minds of spiritual but not religious people.

If you want to row a boat in a straight line, you cannot have unequal amounts of pressure or strength on the oars. To row a boat in a straight line requires careful attention and uniform distribution. As you know, the more power you exert on either oar results in turning one way or the other. The church is like this, actually. We want to be both relevant and countercultural. We must put equal and the right kind of distribution on the oars in order to row in the right direction.

If you don't like the boat analogy, then think of a teeter-totter on a playground. In order to balance, you must have equal weight distribution. How well is your church doing at being relevant and countercultural—100% of both?

I think the balancing force equally distributing the power or influence between the narrative of relevance and the narrative of counterculture is transcendence. The way we become more relevant and countercultural at the same time is by creating environments where people (emerging generations in particular) who are spiritual but not religious can locate transcendence. We create these environments, both inside the walls of the church and outside the walls of the church, by living garden-like lives that are marked by power, peace, provision, and presence.

If we are going to reach and engage emerging generations with the gospel that transcends, it must be done through a communal and individual effort that provides a deep sense of awe, shalom, life, and intimacy.

SIGNALS OF TRANSCENDENCE

In 1969, Peter L. Berger wrote a book called, *A Rumor of Angels: Modern Society and the Rediscovery of the Supernatural*. The book has helped shape the way I think and feel about the notion of transcendence and its influence to bring spiritual people into the church family—not merely so our churches can grow numerically, but so nonreligious people will consider our churches to be garden-like communities shaped by God's power, peace, provision, and presence. It is my hope that in order to partner with the Holy Spirit to help make earth look more like heaven, as we await the day in which all things are made new, that churches and their leaders will move toward establishing garden-like environments where they work, live, and play.

Berger's suggestion is that those in the theological world (such as places of worship and communities of faith) seek out what he calls signals of transcendence. Signals of transcendence, according to Berger, are

" . . . phenomena that are to be found within the domain of our 'natural' reality but that appear to point beyond that reality. In other words, I am not using transcendence here in a technical philosophical sense but literally, as the transcending of the normal, everyday world that I earlier identified with the notion of the 'supernatural.' "[46]

Berger continues by suggesting that there are prototypical human gestures that make up these signals of transcendence. These gestures are actions and experiences that express the essential composition of humans and that are not buried deep into the unconscious mind, but instead belong to the ordinary everyday awareness. Think of this ordinary everyday awareness as signals or signs of transcendence—order, play, hope, courage, and humor, to name a few.

Berger's thesis is that within the ordinary everyday life, all around us there are moments and experiences when we must pause to identify that something otherworldly is at work. This is what I mean by the four P's—power, peace, provision, and presence as a pattern for transcendence. If the church wants to reach and engage Millennials and Generation Z, it must do so through sharing ordinary life with people, but stopping long enough to recognize and attend to the experiences that take an ordinary life into a sphere of the extraordinary.

Let me illustrate this for you. As I have already mentioned in a previous chapter, I coach baseball (actually I coach kids, not the sport). I have a twelve-and-under team that I have been coaching for the past several years. Part of my ministry to the community is coaching this team. I love these kids, parents, and fellow coaches. Through the course of the year, including indoor offseason workouts, practices, tournaments, and league games, it isn't an exaggeration to say that I spend more than five hundred hours a year with these kids. That is roughly twenty days a year. That means that of the 365 days in 2017, the year in which I am writing this book, I will have spent twenty of those days with my team!

This means, obviously, that I get to know the players, parents, and coaches really well. We develop a routine or an ordinary aspect to our lives—practice, game, practice, tournament, practice, game, practice, tournament, and so on and so on. One day a few years ago, one of the parents on my team asked me, "Why do you love these kids so much? They aren't even your kids!" My response was simply, "I believe the way toward a better future are kids who believe in themselves, know how to

---

46. Peter Berger, *A Rumor of Angels: Modern Society and the Rediscovery of the Supernatural* (Anchor Books, Garden City, NJ. 1970), 53.

solve problems, and know how to work together as a team to do so." The parent smiled, shook her head, got back in the car, waved to me, and drove off. That was a moment or a signal of transcendence. Something about my life and her life and the ordinary routine we had developed was shattered by her perplexity as to why I would give up so much time, energy, and money to hang out with kids who weren't even my own.

These signals of transcendence are everywhere. These signals are spiritual moments when the soul is stirred, and these moments take people into a realm of the supernatural that is occasional and maybe even rare. These spiritual experiences, however, are precisely what emerging generations (and all generations, really) are looking for. To be spiritual but not religious is to prove that God is real by living a garden-like life designed by God, modeled by Jesus, and guided by the Holy Spirit. This reality of God is found among the signals of transcendence around us every day, or maybe better said, whispered by rumors of angels, as Berger claims.

FOUR MAJOR BIBLICAL NARRATIVES OF TRANSCENDENCE

Let's take a look at four major events in the Bible that help us to see how the ordinary is interrupted, resulting in a transcendent experience. Transcendent experiences or events are moments in our lives in which something supernatural occurs and we are led to discover something that directs our thinking, feeling, and being beyond natural reality.

One night a few months ago, I decided to leave my return airline ticket unused and chose to drive from Denver, where I had been speaking at a conference, back home where I live in Kansas City. Sometimes I just get tired of the hustle and bustle of airports, so I decided to rent a car and drive the seven hours home at my own pace and in solitude.

For many miles, I drove in a straight line. If you have ever driven through eastern Colorado into western Kansas, you know how flat and straight the highway is. I was moving along at the maximum speed after driving what felt like hundreds of miles in a straight line, when out of nowhere I was met with a ladder in the middle of the road. It wasn't until I was nearly on top of the ladder that I could see the reflection from my headlights onto the shiny aluminum ladder.

Fortunately, no one else was on the road near me so I was able to quickly swerve out of the way to avoid running over the ladder. My heart was racing, and my grip on the steering wheel was a little tighter the next ten miles or so. What was so ordinary—driving straight for miles and miles— was interrupted in seconds, and I was met with a split-second decision to make. The decision I made was the right decision, but the only thing I could think of for the next ten miles or so was what it would have meant for me had I hit that ladder; the near miss pointed to a reality I really didn't want to think about. Could I have swerved into another car? Could I have gotten a flat tire? Could I have swerved off the side of the road and rolled down the embankment? All of those, of course, could have happened had the circumstances been different.

Think of these four major biblical events like this—not so much the potential results, but the ordinary to new-reality moment. Life is sometimes like driving on a flat and straight highway for miles and then, all of a sudden . . . bam! . . . a new reality is upon you.

Since God's power, peace, provision, and presence is seen throughout all of the Bible, it is easy to spot places where humanity experiences the transcendent—taking them beyond the ordinary and into a new reality. For the purposes of this book, I have chosen four major stories from the Bible to help shape our thinking, feeling, and being. In each of these stories, the characters ask a question. It is in asking these questions, I contend, that we are alerted to a human experiencing the natural world exploding into the supernatural—going from ordinary to extraordinary. These four major Bible events are:

1. Moses and the burning bush (Exodus 3:1-21)
2. Jesus calms the storm (Matthew 8:27; Mark 4:39; Luke 8:22-25)
3. Pilate interacting with Jesus during his trial (John 18:28–19:15)
4. Saul's conversion away from a murderous profession (Acts 9)

MOSES AND THE BURNING BUSH—WHAT IS HIS NAME?

This is an event many of us remember from our childhood—a Sunday school classic.

Moses is tending to his father's-in-law flock of sheep when an angel of the Lord appears to Moses in the fire from within a bush. Of course, like any one of us would have done, Moses, filled with awe and a deep interest, makes his way to the bush to see the strange sight—why the bush was on fire but not burning up.

As Moses reaches the bush, God calls, "Moses, Moses!" Moses' response is very simply, "I'm here." "Take off your sandals," God says, "because you are standing on holy ground." After God's identity is revealed, Moses looks away, hiding his face, realizing that he is in God's presence. Struck by an overwhelming awe, Moses knows he is unworthy to be in the presence of God's holy power, and out of a deep sense of reverence, Moses must look away.

After some discussion regarding the oppression of the Israelites and God's desire to exercise God's grace and mercy to rescue them, God commissions Moses to be the one to lead the people out of the hands of an angry Pharaoh.

Five times Moses works to get himself out of a job. Through a series of questions and statements, Moses makes a case for (1) his inadequacy in his and others' eyes to carry out the massive work [3:11], (2) lack of knowledge of who God is [3:13-22], (3) trust that his own won't believe and receive him [4:1-9], (4) the fact that he is not a public speaker [4:12], and (5) request to send another [4:13]. Moses is God's man for the task at hand—to lead God's people out of oppression and into a life God has promised.

Through the series of conversations between God and Moses, clearly Moses is in the midst of a transcendent experience. The bush is on fire, but it isn't consumed? God knows Moses' name? Moses speaks to the mighty God, hidden face and all? Moses, although he tries to escape the job, learns that God is present with him? Moses' question in verse 13, "What's this God's name?" is essential. Moses is searching not only for the name of the one sending him, but also for assurance that Moses is speaking to whom he thinks he is speaking. Moses is assured through this experience of God's power, peace, provision, and presence.

JESUS CALMS THE STORM—WHO IS THIS MAN?

Much like the narrative of Moses' transcendent experience, the disciples, faced with the dangers of a sudden storm on the Sea of Galilee, experience God's power, peace, provision, and presence all in one experience. Many scholars believe it isn't the lack of faith that Jesus will rescue them from the storm that Jesus scolds his followers for. Instead, many believe that Jesus scolds his followers for the lack of belief in what

Jesus has already done that proves he is the Messiah and, therefore, should already know that God will not allow anything to happen to his Son.

"Who then is this?" they ask. "Even the wind and the sea obey him!" (Mark 4:41). Clearly, this is a transcendent moment for the disciples. The power of God is displayed in Jesus calming the storm. The peace of God is displayed in the aftereffects of the storm settling. God's provision of life is spared in the miraculous work of Jesus, and God's presence is with them, quite literally, as Jesus is on the boat.

Moments of transcendence cause us to ask questions like, "Who is this man?" We are stirred, knowing that something beyond the ordinary has taken place amidst the ordinary. Due to the Sea of Galilee being below sea level and the wind generated from the way in which the currents flowed in and around the mountains, it would regularly kick up a squall on the water. The storm was quite ordinary. However, the calming of the storm was not so ordinary. That was extraordinary!

PILATE INTERACTING WITH JESUS DURING HIS TRIAL— WHERE ARE YOU FROM?

Pilate was always in some sort of trouble with the Roman Emperor. At several points in Pilate's career as governor, he was reprimanded for his decisions. The trial of Jesus was no exception. Scholars will tell you that after the crucifixion of Jesus, the emperor summoned Pilate to Rome to give account to the darkness that fell over the earth. Even Pilate's wife, knowing of his not-so-stellar leadership, counseled Pilate to leave Jesus alone.

The hearings of Jesus—in front of Jewish authorities and then Roman authorities—gave Pilate a lot of information with which to think about his decision. From the hearings in front of Annas, Caiaphas, the Sanhedrin, Pilate, Herod, and then back, was a progression that ultimately led Pilate to make the decision he did.

Pilate really didn't care what the religious leaders thought because he knew Jesus was innocent. Although, even with the truth made known to him, Pilate realizes his job performance could not withstand another blemish. So under the pressure, he finally gave in out of an interest in preserving his job and ordered Jesus to be killed. Along the way, however,

Pilate experienced a transcendent moment. In verse 9 of John 19, Pilate asks Jesus, "Where are you from?" Jesus doesn't respond to Pilate's question, which leads me to believe that Pilate was asking in amazement and bewilderment, and likely even in admiration. "Where are you from?" indicates that Pilate knew something was different about Jesus. I am convinced that this was a transcendent moment for Pilate.

When we use the question, "Where are you from?" today, it might also be said, "What planet are you from?" or "Why are you so different?" or "What is it about you?" God's power, peace, provision, and presence is standing right before Pilate in one person, Jesus. Pilate was used to sentencing criminals to death. Sentencing criminals to death is one of the many things the Romans were known to do the best. Sentencing criminals was ordinary. Sentencing Jesus was beyond the ordinary and caused Pilate to shake his head in wonder and marvel and ask, "Where are you from?"

SAUL'S CONVERSION AWAY FROM A MURDEROUS PROFESSION—WHO ARE YOU, SIR?

Saul is on the road to Damascus to find Christians—or, at the time, people who were of "The Way"—and persecute them. Saul's mission was to protect the Jewish religion at all costs, and this meant breathing murderous threats and taking captive anyone who was not upholding the law as passed down from generation to generation.

With orders in hand, Saul is on his way to persecute when he meets the risen Jesus. Jesus appears in an encircling light from heaven. Saul falls to the ground and hears a voice asking him, "Saul, Saul, why are you harassing me?" Saul, completely unaware of who is speaking to him but fully aware that this is a moment beyond the ordinary, responds by asking, "Who are you, Lord?" which might actually be better translated as, "Who are you, Sir?"

Jesus answers Saul by saying, "I am Jesus, whom you are harassing," and Jesus continues by giving orders to Saul to go into the city. The posse with Saul could only stand idly and silently by. The Scriptures say that those with Saul stood "speechless" because they heard something but saw nothing. Blinded and undoubtedly shuddering from the experience, Saul is led into the city per Jesus' instruction.

This event was clearly a massively transcendent experience for all—especially Paul. Like Moses, the disciples, and Pilate, Paul is left with a profound question of, "Who are you?" God's power was in the voice and the light. God's peace is established (verse 31) as the church throughout Judea, Galilee, and Samaria enjoyed a time of peace and strengthening. God's provision to Paul is a new life and mission. God's provision to the church was encouragement and growth. God's presence was clearly in the mix as Jesus spoke directly to Saul, and in the fact that Paul's preaching in Damascus led Barnabas to vouch for Paul's conversion. This transcendent experience was the definitive experience in the life of Paul as it comes up in chapter 22 and also in chapter 26 of Acts.

This book is about reaching and engaging Millennials and Generation Z with the gospel. It is about proclaiming, performing, and making present a gospel that displays God's power, peace, provision, and presence. In the end, this book argues that the one blatantly missing component to the way in which the church proclaims, performs, and makes the gospel present is transcendence.

The way in which the church should go about helping people ask "Who are you?"-type questions is by equally distributing the weight on either end of the teeter-totter, balancing the narratives of relevance and counterculture. That way, in the ordinary, garden-like lives that we as Christians live, we cultivate environments where people can experience and embrace the transcendence of God.

Let me remind you that to live countercultural lives is not to live with the agenda to fix culture's many problems, so to speak, but to allow the Spirit to transform our inner life and outer life, changing the way we choose to live in culture. This is what it means to be in the world but not of the world.

These garden-like environments must be characterized by key traits that can actually cultivate garden-like lives and relationships. Ten of the key garden-like environmental traits we must nurture for people to experience transcendence in the midst of an ordinary life are, in no particular order:

1. **Diligence**—lasting relationships are difficult to nurture if you do not plan on the relationship being built on patience.

2. **Sensitivity**—there are always issues in people's lives in which certain emotions and feelings are heightened.

3. **Empathy**—concern for the other is a must. If there isn't a sincere concern for the others in your life, there will be no others in your life.

4. **Story-sharing/Invitation**—whether a spoken word or through nonverbal cues, there must be an invitation given for someone to have access to your life.

5. **Unrestricted dialogue**—there can never be a topic of conversation that is off limits to discuss. Politics, religion, racism, capitalism, and so forth must be free to converse about for there to be true freedom for the other person's interests.

6. **Patience**—It can take months, years, and even decades for relationships to generate the kinds of conversation necessary to nurture a garden-like environment.

7. **Responsibility**—relationships that are responsible carry with them both accountability and authority. This means that we hold and are held to our words, actions, and promises, and have the ability to call one another out when necessary.

8. **Practice**—relationships that help cultivate garden-like environments have healthy habits in which those sharing their story and community readily make a priority. Some of these habits or practices are respect, service, encouraging words, appreciation, quality time, teamwork, proximity, and time.

9. **Conflict resolution**—every relationship has a struggle or two—suspicion, disagreements, differing opinions, and so forth. A garden-like environment that nurtures potential signals of transcendence has built-in devices to resolve debates and differences.

10. **Affinity**—there is a certain like-mindedness that often parallels deep and meaningful friendships. Determine the matters or issues in the relationship that you share with another and allow that to be one of the anchors of a growing, healthy, and shared life.

Here is the bottom line. We must live in such a way—with, for, and because of others—that resembles the garden-like life that we see in Eden, the garden of Jesus' tomb, and the garden of the new city. The best gospel we can proclaim, perform, and make present is a gospel in which God's power, peace, provision, and presence exist, and where one or more of the attributes of God are reflected and, at any given time, shape our relational contexts.

In the next chapter, we will discuss the prevailing paradigm shifts needed in our churches in order to reach and engage Generation Z with a compelling gospel narrative built upon the garden-like lives we are called to live. If you want to fill up your church with people, you must fill up your lives with people. Don't just make a good impression; make a lifelong invitation—open up your life and share it, knowing that out of lasting relationships, people are formed into better human beings and deeper friends.

The best kinds of lasting relationships are those in which people see each other as friends with no agenda other than life-sharing and constant caring. I have many non-Christian friends, and with all of them are at the point of echoing many or all of the ten characteristics of a garden-like environment listed above. I have had deep conversations about faith in Jesus and my pursuit to live other-than-empire values, driven by the virtues of the kingdom of God.

CHAPTER 5

ASSET-BASED COMMUNITY DISCIPLESHIP

Community developers, those who bring people from local communities together to generate ideas for lasting solutions to common problems and to improve the community by making it sustainably stronger, have a method of bringing about community resilience called, Asset-Based Community Development (ABCD). ABCD is the method whereby the unique and particular strengths of the people, property, and programs of the community are uncovered and organized, and then deployed. This process is done in such a way that the assets of people are the key factors involved in pulling the local communities together to overcome the society's contextual challenges.

Experts in the discipline will tell you that empowering people as individuals and groups in order to affect change in the community is successful when four essential aspects of the community are healthy and flourishing. Those four essential aspects are healthcare, housing, employment, and education. When the assets are discovered amidst the community and leveraged in order to bring people together, it levels the playing field, so to speak, with people of power and ordinary people and, together, can bring about the social reforms needed from entire communities to thrive.

When you think about it, the church is like this. People have assets, such as skills, gifts, talents, experiences, networks, resources, and so forth, and when those assets are found in people and those people are empowered to use them in creative ways, it can create a church that flourishes in the community.

I believe that one of the most important ways of thinking for churches to thrive in the post-Christian context in which we currently live is to develop a strategy that deploys the people from within the church to go outside of the church for what I refer to as *asset-based community discipleship*.

Asset-based community discipleship is simply bringing people from the church and the public together in everyday relational life-sharing situations—most likely but not always exclusively outside the walls of the church—to generate a genuine interest, authentic invitation, and ongoing investment in nonreligious but spiritual people in order to help them find and follow Jesus. Asset-based community discipleship is missional—it sends people from within the church out into culture to cultivate a garden-like life in the way of Jesus.

I recently visited a large Sunday school class at a local church near where I live in Kansas City. The class was comprised of about one hundred people. These one hundred people or so were in their late fifties up into their early eighties. As much as any group of people I have spoken to or consulted with over the last few years, this group was filled with passion to reach younger people. After I had finished presenting my material, the questions were coming fast and furious. I couldn't even begin to address one of the questions before I was met with another. The interest in reaching younger people was life-giving, to say the least.

After about forty minutes of answering and responding to the group's questions, I was finally met with the question that always tops them all. That question is, "So what are we supposed to do with the information now?" Before I could even begin to answer, a woman who looked to be in her late sixties to early seventies simply said, "We are supposed to live like Jesus did. We are supposed to get out of this church—maybe even out of this class once in a while—and take Jesus' message to the people." My heart leapt, and I can only imagine the size of the smile on my face when I heard her response. Another person blurted out, "It always goes back to Jesus."

It really is that simple. It does always go back to Jesus. Jesus was the master of asset-based community discipleship. He called ordinary, average, everyday, and hard-working blue-collar kinds of young men to follow him—not to just walk behind him either, but to imitate him. Jesus taught them what it means to be a servant and to live an inverted, upside-down, backward kind of life. Jesus took these everyday young men and turned them into passionate, faithful, and submissive servants who understood that a simple invitation to follow Jesus was all it took to bring people from various communities forward to participate in God's imaginative and impactful Kingdom life.

As we have already determined, we are living in a post-Christian context. In many ways, our day is like that of the day of Jesus. Jesus' day was pre-Christian, in the sense that it was marked by syncretism, or the acceptance of any and all religious beliefs and teachings due to Roman rule. Outside of the monotheistic Jewish faith was a faith based on polytheism where idols and images were worshipped. The culture in first-century Israel was very spiritual, and the people were very interested in the supernatural or transcendent experiences. To me, first-century life and twenty-first-century life sound similar. Pre- or post-Christian, either way, the thinking of most people is without Jesus.

Today is the day for the church to renew an AD 30 kind of Christianity, where the supernatural act of the Incarnation is widely lived and captivates the imagination of nonreligious people. It is time for the church to send people out into the community to live a garden-like life that seeks to spread a message that produces an interest, invitation, and an investment of people to find and follow Jesus. In order to do this, of course, we must shift some paradigms. Just as the ABCD discipline in the community has four elements that make communities strong and thriving, so, too, does asset-based community discipleship. The four essential paradigms we must shift and continue to shift in order to arrive at a more Jesus-like way in our post-Christian contexts are (1) mission, (2) evangelism, (3) holiness, and (4) leadership. Once shifted or along the way of shifting, these four elements become pillars that hold up our churches.

Asset-based community discipleship is very simply the equipping and sending of people from within our church community—individuals and groups—to cultivate garden-like lives that spark an interest and lead to an unending invitation and commitment to a long-term investment in people for the sake of the world.

TOWARD NEW PARADIGMS

I don't lead a church; I lead within a church. I work within the construct of a 27-plus-year-old church—a thriving church community that has a long-standing commitment to the four pillars of asset-based community discipleship. We may not refer to it as an ABCD church, necessarily, but sometime along the way, I realized that is what it is—a church that discovers the assets of people and deploys them around the city, country, and globe for the purpose of making disciples who are deeply committed. These four pillars of mission, evangelism, holiness, and leadership are not only something lead pastors need to develop, but also any supporting staff like myself who are in roles that help the senior leadership accomplish the purpose and vision.

After I had finished speaking at a recent conference, this group of young pastors asked me to lunch. The first question they asked was related to my job and what it is like to serve at such a large and growing church. The second question they asked was, "How do we shift toward the four paradigms you mentioned in your presentation, when we are not in charge of the church?" That, of course, is a fair question. Therefore, before I flesh out what I think it takes to make the movement toward what I believe are the four pillars necessary to develop a faith community that consists of a commitment to asset-based community discipleship, I want to address that question in detail.

Some of you reading this are not in charge or feel as thought you don't have any authority or power to make the necessary decisions to take this concept widespread in your church. I get that. I am fortunate in that I serve in a church that has a commitment to the four pillars already. We are always looking for ways to deepen our commitment, but I don't have to change the culture, as the discipleship culture already exists—my job is to help resource and guide people to live the four pillars more faithfully in the community.

Through our men's ministry, our women's ministry, our small groups, our young adults' ministry, our ministry to boomers, our Sunday school classes, our learning events, and our curriculum, I am always trying to find ways (along with my fantastic staff) to call more people into our discipleship environments and equip them with the tools needed to make disciples in our community.

The great thing about these four pillars is that they are straight from life and the ministry of Jesus. We don't need to have our church councils and elder boards adopt a new resolution in order to make these a reality in our churches. Honestly, all we have to do is live it personally, equip people toward the development of them, and then release people to use their assets to be the church in the community and disciple others.

You do not need to be in charge to implement these shifts; you just need to be committed to them and committed to seeing them made real in your church—even if it is one person at a time or one department at a time. Sometimes I think that although we work within the framework of an already existing church vision and structure, we don't think we have the freedom to lead. Sometimes we forget that as Christians, the Holy Spirit is within us, guiding us and giving us the power to be the witnesses we are called to be.

So for those of you who are wrestling with how to make change in your particular church—stop over-thinking it. If you faithfully live the values you want to see become widespread in passionate and compelling ways, giving people an imagination for what it can look like in their lives, it'll become a reality. It may take more time than you ever thought it would, but this is how the reproduction of disciples works—it is contagious. This, of course, does not mean that we don't need to be and become better strategic and tactical leaders. It does mean, however, as a vocational minister—whether clergy or lay staff or a volunteer—you've already been empowered to lead within the makeup of the Great Commission.

As we lead, we need to help people discover or rediscover the four essential pillars of asset-based community discipleship. As humble servants, desiring to connect with spiritual but not religious people—particularly emerging generations—we need to lead with a commitment to faithful, generous, and hope-centered leadership that transfers the power to the people of our communities and equips, challenges, and inspires them to go and make disciples.

A SHIFT IN OUR MISSIONAL THINKING[47]

Before we can truly understand missional thinking and modeling, we must first understand and possess a robust narrative theology. In what's probably its simplest definition, narrative theology is conversation about God in the setting of a story. We know this story as the Bible.

---

47. Thoughts on pages 83–97 are adapted from a previous book I wrote, *Story Signs and Sacred Rhythms: A Narrative Approach to Youth Ministry*. I have merely adapted some of the content of that book to bring greater context to how we shift our missional mindset and thinking to reach and engage emerging generations.

Narrative theology in its three integrative aspects of biblical text, faith communities, and cultural contexts is perhaps the broadest way in which to understand God. It's "an account of characters and events in a plot moving over time and space through conflict toward resolution."[48]

Narrative theology is primarily about exactly what you might assume: story and doctrine. However, narrative theology is more than a mere story. Without the accompanying doctrine that intends to point to and signify the reality of God, the narrative of God would have no more authority nor hold any more truth than some of the greatest stories ever written. And the doctrine within the story is more than just a collection of propositions as well. As Charles Van Engen so clearly states in *Mission on the Way*, narrative theology is "broader and deeper than dogmatic propositions."[49] Van Engen gives us four reasons why narrative theology is more than propositions.

First, narrative theology accounts for a community of faith. This means that the narrative of God is also a story about people. Clearly the people of Israel and the early church are major indicators of who God is throughout the entire narrative. One can suppose, therefore, that God wishes to reveal not only God to generations coming and going, but also what it means for humanity to work together to live in the intended ways of God.

Second, Van Engen offers this: God places God in the midst of human history. Theology isn't meant to be a distant set of theories and speculations. Rather, theology is very much about how God interacts with people to form human history. Narrative theology is not only about a community of God's people, but also about how God and God's people interrelate. From the beginning of the story, we see God's passion for relationship and intimacy with God's creation. Therefore, we might conclude that narrative theology is bigger than a set of propositions, as propositions are often so closed.

Third, narrative theology is about being on a "faith pilgrimage." God's revelation is as much about the spirituality of a wandering people as it is about God's propositions. God chooses to reveal the journey God shared with the people of Israel and the church to call others to be pilgrim people—people on the move who are traveling as God leads them, not as they desire to go. Far too often in our youth ministries, we neglect the concept of pilgrimage. We talk incessantly about faith being a

---

48. Charles Van Engen, *Mission on the Way: Issues in Mission Theology* (Baker Academic, Grand Rapids, MI. 1996), 54.
49. Ibid, 55.

journey—and rightfully so. But seldom do we connect the journey of faith with God's direction of us—as both individuals and as a community of travelers.

And for me, the word *journey* doesn't encapsulate the holy wandering of a holy people quite like the word *pilgrimage* does. A journey is a trip, expedition, voyage, passage, and so on. A pilgrimage is also a trip, but it's a trip leading to a special place—a sacred place characterized by wholeness and restoration.

Narrative theology calls God's people to a life of pilgrimage—a life of holy wandering in which the mystical and mysterious hold as much worth as stability and security. We're all on a pilgrimage into the unknown, and the only way to survive is to trust God.

Finally, Van Engen suggests that narrative theology integrates God's words and actions. Furthermore, it allows for the actions of God to give context, meaning, and significance to the words God speaks and the interchange between God and humanity. So narrative theology guides us away from the act of separating God's actions and words, and toward viewing them as being interrelated.

Narrative theology is, compared to other types of theology, constructed around a fuller and more robust idea of God that comes from God's enduring, unfolding drama. Juxtaposed to reducing ideas and concepts of God into clean and effortlessly understood categories or propositions, narrative theology is a broad but accurate and pointed construct of God that's more messy than clean and requires more effort to form abstract thoughts about God. Narrative theology finds its meaning in stories, knowing that humans are people of story—God's story. As Van Engen writes, "Systematic theology engages the intellect; storytelling engages the heart and indeed the whole person."[50]

Too often, enthusiastic and hurried leaders lead people in an intellectual game of leapfrog from the story of God directly into the propositions of God, thereby missing the most important aspect of theology altogether— how we allow it to shape and direct our lives.

---

50. Ibid, 52.

Such leaping creates a hole that some people will never have the opportunity to fill. Before you can legitimize proposition, you have to first legitimize story. Propositions are found throughout the Bible. However, it's sloppy theology to examine propositions without first finding their meaning within the story itself. Therefore, in order to most effectively and efficiently guide people into discipleship, we must first consider the greater context in which the propositions are found.

THE RISKS AND REWARDS ASSOCIATED WITH NARRATIVE THEOLOGY

Several years ago, I was in Southeast Asia to attend a meeting of leaders from various youth ministry organizations from around the globe. During one of our sessions, one leader said, "I think we should just teach from the Gospels. Any other text that we teach from just confuses kids." I couldn't believe what I'd heard. I was floored that anyone could make such a statement.

Unfortunately, as I've traveled to various places since then, I've found that while people rarely say it as boldly as that gentleman did, they still function that way, and most churches are almost exclusively teaching Jesus only through the lens of the Gospel narratives. That kind of teaching isn't narrative theology. Narrative theology, like any story, brings context and meaning. Without the greater story, there's no context of who Jesus is, therefore, there's certainly no meaning of Jesus being thrust into the character of our church.

I believe systematic theology, as with most theological constructs, can be helpful. However, I don't believe that a systematic theology that is void of its true narrative context is the best place to start a comprehensive and inclusive study of God. When we start with systematic theology, we may encounter the following hazards:

- We risk missing God's mission to restore the world, as revealed through God's interrelated, overarching meta-narrative.

- We risk being tempted to contrive concepts of God just to fit them into neat, clean, and easily understood divisions.

- We risk missing the global and local context(s) in which Scripture is given to us and in which it's best understood.

- We risk missing what theologians and scholars throughout history have said about God and led others to believe.

- We risk being closed-minded and, therefore, afraid of new discoveries and concepts about God that come with a harmonious open-mindedness and imagination.

- We risk simply indoctrinating ourselves and our entire church with information about God, instead of providing experiential or applied theology that leads to a Christian formation and union with God.

- We risk avoiding the application of God's truths to our modern-day social issues and concerns, which therefore are found by many to be irrelevant.

Therefore, I believe it makes more sense and has a much greater impact when we look at God through the lens of narrative theology. When we do so, we're bound to find the following rewards:

- The unity of the narrative—The parts of God's story are interrelated and interconnected, thus we find unity in God's entire story. We don't find meaning in Jesus or the gospel or Pentecost or the Flood or the Tower of Babel or the crossing of the Red Sea or any narrative, unless we view it in relationship to all of the narratives.

- The universalism of the narrative—Just as the various narratives connect to give meaning to a greater whole, so the narrative provides history for a larger context. The Bible wasn't written for one particular faith heritage or group of people. The Bible was written for all people and for all times, and this makes it unequivocally universal.

- The uncovering of God within the narrative—It's in the unity and universalism of God's narrative that we see the most of God. In the Bible, we see the overarching idea and makeup of God, as well as the mighty acts of God. These mighty acts reveal God as a God of power, strength, faithfulness, and so on. It's in the unity of the narrative and its universalism, then, that we see God's mighty work displayed in Jesus.

- The uncovering of the Christ-centered nature of the narrative—Without Jesus, the story of God remains just as incomprehensible as Jesus would be without God. Jesus Christ is the whole point of the story. Jesus and the restorative actions of his person and work is, in fact, the open secret of God. This "open secret" is available to any who wish to welcome it, yet it's a secret to those who don't know about Jesus. This is why God's missionary heart needs to be revealed through the work of God's mission.

FROM NARRATIVE TO MISSION

Mission comes out of one place—God's heart. Mission is an attribute of God that's best understood from God's narrative. God is a missionary God and, therefore, mission must be seen as God's movement into the world. That's the exact opposite of how it's often viewed, which is that mission is the primary activity of the church.

David Bosch writes, "There is church because there is mission, not vice versa."[51] Of course, the church plays a huge role in the mission of God, but the mission of God isn't something the church does; it's simply who God is. Our work is to join God in carrying out God's mission, not manufacture our own mission.

Christopher Wright, author of *The Mission of God: Unlocking the Bible's Grand Narrative,* says, "Fundamentally, our mission (if it is biblically informed and validated) means our committed participation as God's people, at God's invitation and command, in God's own mission within history of God's world for the redemption of God's creation."[52] It can be understood from Wright's definition of mission, therefore, that discipleship is our attempt through God's design for the church to participate in God's mission to restore the world.

Mission is important to leaders for several reasons. First, the mission of God gives us a reason. Sometimes we can get lost in the details of all that we do, and it's easy to take our eyes off God and put them on the things surrounding us.

Second, the missio Dei is important because it gives both focus and purpose. We aren't needed to be people of our own dreams. Our dreams and our desires to see those dreams accomplished are far from wrong. However, at the end of the day, we disciple people because God is a missionary God who longs to see the world God created as "very good" return to its intended condition of wholeness—that's God's dream.

---

51. David Bosch, *Transforming Mission: Paradigm Shifts in Theology of Mission* (Orbis Books, Maryknoll, NY. 1994), 390.

52. Christopher Wright, *The Mission of God: Unlocking the Bible's Grand Narrative* (Intervarsity Press, Downers Grove, IL. 2006), 234.

Third, mission work is God's. Remembering this fact takes the pressure off of us. We shouldn't become complacent, but the world isn't ours to win—it's God's. We don't conquer the world and lay it at God's feet, saying, "Look what we've done for you!" Rather, we ought to lay ourselves at God's feet and say, "Look at what you've done for me, with me, and through me."

Fourth, the missio Dei is important to leaders because it provides the framework in which we view God's activity. This means we do not need to scurry around and look for ways to structure a ministry platform out of nothing. We look to God—through God's narrative—to see a mission that's already at work. Therefore, we aren't needed to "drum up business" for the mission, but rather find where God is already working and join God there.

Finally, the missio Dei is important because the mission is the message. In other words, the mission of God articulates the good news that God is a God-for-people. One of the most important aspects of mission is evangelism—proclaiming Jesus Christ as Savior. The proclamation of salvation—or what I refer to as the message of the mission—calls people to repentance and conversion. It calls people to receive or take hold of God's forgiveness, become members of a new community, and begin a life of ministry in the way of Jesus that's powered by and through the Holy Spirit. Leaders need not worry about creating a message—the message of the mission is already here. And this truth allows you to be creative in other areas.

It's important to remember that the practice of the mission is carried out in a broken world. The message of the mission is simple, but that doesn't mean it's easy. We live in the tension between God's purpose, plan, and providence, and humanity's confusion, doubt, and uncertainty. It's important to not only recognize that tension, but also live in it with certainty and calm, knowing that out of an informed balance, we bring the message of the mission to our church and community, and God's compassionate work of the Holy Spirit will do the rest.

FOUR P'S OF GOD'S MISSION

Lesslie Newbigin was a theologian and missiologist. While spending many years in India as a missionary, Newbigin was heavily involved in helping people understand God's mission through his teaching and writing. *The Open Secret: An Introduction to the Theology of Mission* was just one of his many works that concisely outlined the mission of God and the message of it in the culture.

To Newbigin, the mission is about God *proclaiming* the Kingdom, Jesus making the Kingdom *present* among God's people, and the *prevenience* (previousness) of the Kingdom through the Holy Spirit. In other words, the mission of God forms the context of the person and work of Jesus. Jesus reveals the mission of God to the world through his life, teachings, and deeds. Jesus also sends the Spirit to give witness to the mission of God and to equip the church for its mission to participate with God in restoring the world toward its intended wholeness.

Newbigin gives three P words to help us understand the missio Dei: *proclaim, present,* and *prevenience.* I'd like to add a fourth: *practice.* The Holy Spirit equips the church to practice the work of God or to live out the story of God—and our churches need to be about the practice of the mission.

But before we can begin with a comprehensive framework for narrative— missional model of discipleship—it's important that we understand the origin, nature, work, and goals of the mission of God. Discipleship that's living out the heart of God through its missionary activity must deeply realize the correlation between God's mission and the work of our churches.

THE ORIGINS OF THE MISSION OF GOD

We've already established this, but for the sake of review, the mission of God finds its origin in the heart of God. In the words of David Bosch in *Transforming Mission:*

"It cannot be denied that the missio Dei notion has helped to articulate the conviction that neither the church nor any other human agent can ever be considered the author or bearer of mission. Mission is, primarily and ultimately, the work of the Triune God, Creator, Redeemer, and Sanctifier, for the sake of the world, a ministry in which the church is privileged to participate. . . . Mission has its origin in the heart of God. God is a fountain of sending love. This is the deepest source of mission. It is impossible to penetrate deeper still; there is mission because God loves people."[53]

We aren't about our own work. We're exclusively about the work of God—as seen in God's heart, through God's mission, and understood best from God's narrative. The origin of mission has its source in the heart of God, not our church bulletins, websites, or mission statements, which are often based on one verse or proposition. While it's important to contextualize the mission of God, we must keep in mind that the more we try to reduce God into understandable, incremental propositions for our people, the smaller God becomes. And the smaller God becomes, the fewer reasons our people have to accept and then contribute to God's mission of salvation and justice.

I appreciate the words of Charles Van Engen: "Mission is the people of God intentionally crossing barriers from church to nonchurch, faith to nonfaith, to proclaim by word and deed the coming of the kingdom of God in Jesus Christ; this task is achieved by means of the church's participation in God's mission of reconciling people to God, to themselves, to each other, and to the world, and gathering them into the church through repentance and faith in Jesus Christ by the work of the Holy Spirit with a view to the transformation of the world as a sign of the coming kingdom in Jesus Christ."[54]

THE NATURE OF THE MISSION OF GOD

There are three integrative aspects of the nature of the mission of God that must be understood: The *biblical text,* the people of God or *faith communities,* and the *cultural context* in which our individual faith communities and the biblical text intersect—our missional context.

Each of these is imperative to the mission of God and the work that our churches engage to accomplish God's mission. Regardless of the model of ministry, the work of the church is to integrate the culture, the Bible, and the faith community, and ultimately express the heart of God—to restore the world and bring justice to all.

At times it's hard to remember that we don't practice discipleship outside of the culture. For many of us, there's an urge to protect our people from it. Sure, we want the culture to interact with our faith community—we call this "outreach." I contend, however, that culture is just as much a

---

53. David Bosch, *Transforming Mission: Paradigm Shifts in Theology of Mission* (Orbis Books, Maryknoll, NY. 1994), 392.
54. Charles Van Engen, *Mission on the Way: Issues in Mission Theology* (Baker Academic, Grand Rapids, MI. 1996), 29.

part of the mission of God as is the faith community—even as much as Scripture is. In other words, if the nature of the mission of God involves all three, then why do we tend to separate culture from the Bible and the faith community? Our churches must work diligently to integrate all three.

THE WORK OF THE MISSION OF GOD

The work of the mission of God is *evangelism* or proclaiming, performing, and making the gospel present. The church is about the *contextualization* of the gospel. The work of the mission of God is also *liberation*. Our churches must be about setting people free from the constraints that keep them from establishing a restorative relationship with God, themselves, others, and the world. The work of the church is about freeing people from the very things that hold them captive. And the work of proclaiming the gospel is to *impart* the mission into the culture. This isn't a mere contextualization where the mission is made relevantly accessible. Rather, it's about converting the culture from hearers to storytellers of the mission of God.

To jump back to the nature of the mission for a second, this proves how important the culture is to the mission of God and why it can arguably be considered equal to the roles of Scripture and faith communities. If there's no culture, then there's no need to impart the message of the mission. If there's no culture, then to whom are we proclaiming the message of the mission?

THE GOALS OF THE MISSION OF GOD

There are two primary goals of the mission of God, and I've alluded to them already. The two goals of God's mission are *salvation* and *justice*. According to Millard Erickson, in his book *Christian Theology*, "Salvation is a total change in an individual that progresses through sanctification toward glorification."[55] Traditionally, salvation involves regeneration, sanctification, adoption, justification, redemption, reconciliation, and union. Out of these important components, we're able to see signs of new life. What do those signs look like? They include:

• finding fellowship with God and God's people;

• a love for God and God's people;

55. Millard J. Erickson, *Christian Theology* (Baker Academic, Grand Rapids, MI. 1983), 901.

- the proclamation of Jesus as a means of delivering the message of the mission of God;

- ongoing obedience to the intended ways of God and teachings of Scripture;

- committing to do the will of God; and

- yielding to the work and ministry of the Holy Spirit in us and through us.

Our churches are clearly about the work of salvation, but they should also be about the work of justice. Simply said, the work of justice is righting wrongs. While salvation does provide justice in a larger, more comprehensive way, our churches aren't solely about saving souls. In fact, I believe we fall short of God's intended mission to restore the world to its intended wholeness when our agenda contains only the salvation of the soul. We ought to also be about righting the wrongs in our world— bringing a true dignity to all.

The mission of God places us directly in the heart of a broken world where we're to look for ways to care for the physical, emotional, and social needs of those around us, just as much as we're to care for their spiritual needs. Regardless of the outcome of our acts of deep justice, when we care for God's people and God's creation, we warm the missionary heart of God.

It isn't evangelism or justice—it's *both*. They may be separated in task and function at times, but they're never two separate, optional components of the mission of God.

As you know, there are various essential aspects of social concern and justice. In talking with my Catholic friends, I've discovered that the Catholic Church designates seven areas or key themes as it relates to justice (as identified by the United States Conference of Catholic Bishops). Those themes are:

1. Sanctity of human life and dignity of the person;
2. Call to family, community, and participation;
3. Rights and responsibilities [of humanity];
4. Preferential [care] for the poor and vulnerable;
5. Dignity of work and the rights of workers;

6. Solidarity;

7. Care for God's creation.

I believe each of our churches could measure its efforts and effectiveness in the areas of social concern and justice around these seven key themes. In doing so, I believe we could more deeply engage the mission of God specifically to the integration of the Scriptures, the context of our faith communities, and the context of the surrounding culture. And as a result of our growing awareness of areas of concern and ongoing acts of compassion, perhaps we might see the righting of wrongs in such areas as violence elimination, ecology, politics, income redistribution, racial equality, healthcare, urban and rural renewal, fair trade, and an end to modern-day slavery.

For our churches to be about justice, we leaders must first seek to examine our own hearts. Are we compassionate people? Do we care about justice? Why do we care about justice? An examination of the heart will most often lead to a confession of neglect. We recognize the importance of justice, but we often leave it for others to do. Neglect is far too common. Look around you. You'll see people in need today—and not just halfway around the world, but halfway down your block.

But people in need aren't just financially poor and in need of food, money, and clothes. Poverty-stricken people may also be those who need love, respect, care, and friendship. There are people living in my neighborhood who are poor. They may live in 3,000-square-foot homes and have all the money they need, but without love in their lives, they're poor. We need to examine our hearts not only for compassion, but also for respect toward the people we choose to be compassionate to and with.

For our churches to be about justice (along with salvation), we must repent of our neglect just as we'd repent of other sins. We must also begin to stand with the undignified and exploited of this world. It isn't enough for our youth ministry and students to just do acts of service. We must seek active justice by living amid the needs of others.

In *A Glimpse of Jesus: The Stranger to Self-Hatred*, Brennan Manning quotes Barbara Doherty:

"Love is service. There is no point in getting into an argument about this question of loving. It is what Christianity is all about take it or leave it.

Christianity is not about ritual and moral living except insofar as these two express the love that causes both of them. We must at least pray for the grace to become love."[56]

The narrative of God reveals the mission of God. The mission of God reveals the very heart of God. It's through God's heart of love that the work of our churches becomes increasingly clear and incredibly compelling. Churches are to be about the salvation and justice of this world, as determined by God and through the efforts of evangelism, contextualization, liberation, and impartation.

A SUMMARY OF GOD'S MISSION

As I've already mentioned, the mission of God is:

- God the Father (Proclaim) sending the Son (Presence);

- God the Father and the Son sending the Holy Spirit (Prevenience);

- God the Father, the Son, and the Spirit sending the church (Practice) into the world for the purpose of salvation and justice.

If we're going to inspire, challenge, and equip our churches to be about the mission of God, then we must help them discover the characteristics of the mission. It's out of the discovery of God's mission, the formation of a deep connection with it followed by an even deeper commitment to it, that people will engage in the missio Dei.

We've drawn several conclusions about God's mission previously in this chapter. Before moving on to the other key paradigm shifts, I'd like to present a list of twelve essential characteristics of God's mission.

Twelve Essential Characteristics of God's Mission

1. God's mission is fully Trinitarian. There's no question that the mission of God involves all of the Godhead. Without any one of the three Persons, the church which practices the Kingdom work proclaimed by God and made present by Jesus and made able by the Holy Spirit is left to splash around on its own and try to keep its head above water.

2. God's mission is overtly personal. God has called each and every one of us to be a part of God's mission. No one is able to test out or opt

---

56. Brennan Manning, *A Glimpse of Jesus: The Stranger to Self-Hatred* (HarperOne, New York. 2003), 29.

out of it. God's mission is both private and public. It's private because it influences our own spiritual growth and discovery; it's public because it's seen by the world. However private or public, it's personal. God's mission is directly related to each one of us, and it's out of each of our natures and uniquenesses that we carry the mission out into the world.

3. God's mission is explicitly communal. We're each called to be agents of God's restoration, but we don't operate alone. Rather, we function in what's intended to be a deeply united people, a community that's marked by its love, inclusiveness, and belonging—called the church.

4. God's mission is wonderfully holistic. God's mission isn't merely about saving souls. It's about the entirety of a person. This is why we'd define God's mission as having two goals or objectives: *salvation* (the soul) and *justice* (which intends to touch others' social, physical, environmental, and economic needs, as much as their spiritual ones).

5. God's mission is thoughtfully political. By *political*, I don't mean that God's mission has red states and blue states. I do, however, mean that God's mission is intended to reach into all areas of life, including public matters. The mission of God supersedes the common world and makes its way into the affairs of the state, which is why I believe we all should be politically aware and active.

6. God's mission is unequivocally ecumenical. I love the recent unity and partnership I've felt among my friends in other denominations and segments of Christendom. My Catholic friends in Kansas City and beyond are as interested in the mission of God as any of my evangelical or mainline Protestant friends are. The mission of God transcends the theological boundaries that so many of us keep in order to be "right."

7. God's mission is deliberately cooperative. By *cooperative,* I mean that God's mission is a joint mission between God and God's people. I also mean that God's mission isn't just about the church or those who serve in the church. Since God's activity is all around us and we enter into what God is already doing, God's mission can also be found in the schools, in the workplace, in the university, and in the government.

8. God's mission is distinctly Christian. A Christian is one who believes in Jesus Christ and whose life is derived from Jesus' teachings. Therefore, in order for God's mission to be Christian, it must involve the life, voice, deeds, and teachings of Jesus. Oftentimes when we're dealing with the missio Dei, we can lose focus on the proper concept of Jesus. Jesus is the perfect image of God. Without it, we have no one to guide our lives or a way to guide the rest of the world to see God.

9. God's mission is intentionally contextual. The mission of God is best activated when it's pertaining to the context in which we minister. Each of our contexts looks and feels different, but God's mission carries with it a message from Jesus that's transportable into any and all contexts. One isn't more receptive than another.

10. God's mission is enduringly undividable. God's mission can't be separated into parts. In other words, God's mission isn't designed to reflect only certain characteristics of God or teach certain passages of Scripture. The mission of God is a take-all-or-nothing kind of mission. We can probably think of people who use only the parts they like best. If we're honest, we'll even admit to fighting the urge to divide the mission of God into the parts we believe to be the most important. And sure, there are times, depending on the context, when we'll emphasize certain aspects of God's narrative and mission over others. However, that shouldn't be a permanent practice.

11. God's mission is excitingly mysterious. We know God works in mysterious ways. We know the things of God are above us, and God's ways are higher than our ways. Embracing the mystery and wonder of God's mission helps us enthusiastically embrace the unplanned and unpredictable experiences in our church and in our life.

12. God's mission is increasingly expansive. One of the most telling aspects of the mission of God is its expansiveness. The mission of God is real and working. We know this is true because the church, God's agent of mission, is growing both numerically and spiritually. And as the church grows, the mission of God grows. At times, you may not feel as though your particular faith community is growing numerically. However, think about the universal aspect of God's mission and be encouraged!

A SHIFT IN OUR EVANGELISTIC THINKING

No only do we need a shift in the way we think about mission, we need a shift in the way we think about evangelism. This shift should move us away from thinking that evangelism is (1) detached from discipleship, (2) something the pastor/church does instead of me, (3) a growth strategy, and (4) meant to *convince* people to follow Jesus.

Evangelism is a part of discipleship. Jesus didn't do evangelism; he invited people to follow him or to become a disciple. Also, when we look at the five commissions in the Gospels and in the Book of Acts (Matthew 28:19-20; Mark 16:15-16; Luke 24:46-49; John 20:21-22; Acts 1:8), we do not see a push for evangelism specifically. Instead, we see a call to make disciples and to witness to the truth of Jesus by bearing the fruit of the Holy Spirit. Making disciples does mean that we will be people who invite people to follow Jesus or share the good news. This is the invitation that calls people to be lifelong imitators of Jesus, not merely converts. Many Christians I meet in the churches I have the privilege of being in throughout the year when asked what evangelism is, say, "Evangelism is inviting people to believe in Jesus." Yes, this is the invitation or part of it anyway. To "believe" in Jesus is to choose to trust that Jesus is a real person and to commit to a life transformation.

I appreciate how Dr. Hal Knight and Dr. Douglas Powe Jr. define evangelism in their book, *Transforming Evangelism:* "Evangelism is our sharing and inviting others to experience the good news that God loves us and invites us into a transforming relationship through which we are forgiven, receive new life, and are restored to the image of God, which is love."[57] New life is the goal, and this goal is what leads us toward living in such a way that reflects the garden-like life we were meant to live—a life that shines forth the power, peace, provision, and presence of God.

Some of the people I meet, even in our own congregation, see evangelism as something the pastor or church staff should be doing on their behalf. Essentially this is the big-fisherman mentality, as many others and I have called it for years. This mentality goes like this . . . I will invite my family, friends, coworkers, and so forth, to church, and my pastor or staff will reel them in, so to speak. This is not evangelism in the way of the Great Commission. Evangelism is not a campaign; it is a way of life. Each of us Christians has a story to tell—a story that involves our accepting that Jesus does provide salvation and, therefore, we choose to engage a life in which we are converted out of our old self and into the image of love—humility, hope, joy, and wholeness. Please stop inviting your friends to church if you are not going to invite them into your life to experience the

---

57. Henry H. Knight III and F. Douglas Powe, Jr., *Transforming Evangelism: The Wesleyan Way of Sharing Faith* (Discipleship Resources, Nashville, TN. 2006), 17.

transformation as a firsthand witness. Your friends want to hear from you . . . not from someone they don't know.

Evangelism is sometimes seen, because of the campaign-like use of it within churches, as a way to grow your church—a strategy to bring more giving units into the church, to fill the seats, to participate on boards, to serve in Sunday school, and so forth. Yes, it is very true that evangelism, when rightly understood, may lead to the growth of your church. I am as interested and as passionate as anyone about seeing people become Christians. However, I am not as concerned with the number of them who end up coming to my church. Rather, I am concerned with the number of people in my life who experience the goal of evangelism: conversion. This should bring people into our community, but not to pad the stats. This should bring people into our church community to join in the process of conversion that affects everything about us including our ethics, vocations, routines, relationships, and promises.

We do not convince people to follow Jesus. We invite them to follow Jesus, to do what he did, through the example of our own life. Evangelism cannot merely be thought of as convincing someone to rationally or logically follow Jesus. Yes, thinking people need a way to challenge their assumptions and the churches, to wrestle with the claims of the Bible, and to intellectually test and even defy all that they have come to know about life and faith. Evangelism is not about convincing people to follow Jesus. If it is, it will not last. Conversion, that is, will not last. Each day we choose to follow Jesus, and to choose to follow Jesus is to engage deeper in our trusting relationship that leads to our garden-like created existence.

Emerging generations, maybe even more than anyone else, need a bigger idea of the gospel. They need for you and me to share the good news, or the gospel, in ways that capture their imagination and resonate with them. The gardens resonate because they are places filled with awe, wholeness, life, and intimacy. Evangelism, when rightly done, invites people into the garden-like life to create garden-like environments for others. The commitment that emerging generations have for purpose and meaning, the common good and possibility is what the garden is all about. Simply said, evangelism—since, in the end, is about conversion—is really all about creating garden-like settings in which people can experience the power, peace, provision, and presence of God through growth and vibrancy.

If evangelism is not separate from discipleship, something the pastor or church does for a growth strategy, an intellectual exercise that is aimed at convincing people to follow Jesus, then what exactly is it? Emerging generations need for us to get clear on what the gospel is and how we go about sharing this good news. Evangelism must be a clear discipline within each of our churches if we are going to be conduits of Jesus' prayer, to make earth look more like heaven. If we are going to help equip our congregations to live out an asset-based community discipleship, then we must have a clear understanding of what evangelism is. Below are eight key concepts of evangelism that we must help our congregations know and live.

1. **Evangelism is birthed out of mission.** God's mission is to restore the world toward its intended wholeness—to make it garden-like. The way the world is restored is through people believing in Jesus and living a life like Jesus did, in which we live into the image we were created. Inviting people into this life of purpose, good, and possibility is through sharing the good news. Sharing the good news is evangelism, which is ultimately discipleship.

2. **Evangelism is a process.** It is a mistake to think of conversion as one moment. Conversion, or the process of Christian formation, is a progression. The good news that in Jesus Christ there is salvation can quickly become bad news when people imagine that following Jesus is merely a one-time decision. To follow Jesus may involve a moment of transcendence or two or three, and it may mean that a person is aware of their self and makes a decision to experience the freedom new life brings. However, new life is not attained in one decision. Rather, making a daily, often moment-by-moment decision to follow Jesus leads us into a new and transforming life.

3. **Evangelism is forming people into Christians.** A Christian is a person whom Christ is living within. Since evangelism is really just the beginning stages of discipleship, evangelism has a goal to transform people into authentic, deeply committed Christians who bear the fruit of the Holy Spirit. Evangelism is more about becoming like Christ than it is just about being less of a jerk, a better mother or spouse, or employer. Evangelism leads people to live like Jesus lived.

4. **Evangelism points to God's kingdom reign.** God's kingdom reign is the realization that Jesus is the King of our lives. The kingdom of God

is not like all the other earthly and human kingdoms. The kingdom of God is inverted, upside down, and backwards. The kingdom of God is the opposite of empire. As Christ lives in us, the ethics of a selfish empire is pushed back and makes room for a Kingdom that is built on humility, sacrifice, and service.

5. **Evangelism is always contextual.** Many churches do not understand their context. Evangelism, speaking very pragmatically, only works when the people sharing the good news and inviting others into a new life marked by continuous conversion is shared in a way that the culture can understand. If you were going to be a missionary in the classic sense (you are a missionary already, by the way) the first thing you would need to do to take the gospel with you effectively is to learn the language. Evangelism must be shared within the language of the culture or context around you.

6. **Evangelism is a practice of the whole church.** Members and regular attenders of our churches cannot opt out of evangelism. This is the call of every believer—to make disciples of all nations. Just because you didn't score high on the "evangelist" part of the spiritual gifts inventory doesn't mean you have the freedom to opt out of the process. Evangelism is a practice of the whole church, and our job as leaders, as we will discuss later in this chapter, is to equip our congregations with the tools to share the good news that in Jesus Christ there is salvation and justice, contextually, with all that we come into contact with.

7. **Evangelism brings people into a community.** I think you would agree that Christian formation happens best in the midst of authentic community. This means, since evangelism is a part of Christian formation or discipleship, that evangelism that works brings people into the community for the sake of the world. Community is meant for you to be a place where you share your gifts, talents, and skills (assets) with others. Others do the same for you, and this means that within community, there is not one person in need. Evangelism or making disciples must invite people into your community and not leave them hanging to figure out how to live this "new life" on their own.

8. **Evangelism is as much about presence as it is about proclamation and performance.** Jesus was present with people, and through his faithful presence in the lives of others, Jesus was able to proclaim he was the Son of God and perform the signs that pointed to that truth. If

you are unwilling to truly be present with others, then don't share the good news because it won't truly be the good news. A lot of people can talk about Jesus, and a lot of people are happy to do the kinds of things Jesus did—compassionate acts. However, I have found that few people are really ready to invest the time to be present with others.

We need a new kind of evangelism in our churches today. We need an evangelism that seeks to bring people into a community in which, together, everyone is striving to become like Jesus and do the things Jesus did. In particular, emerging generations need for your church to commit to disciple-making, which includes evangelism. Some churches are great at forming people into Christ, and other churches are great at inviting people to follow Jesus. The truth of it, however, is that they both go hand in hand. We need to rethink the way we communicate what evangelism is and make sure that our congregants see evangelism as outlined above. If we want to reach emerging generations, our churches will need to get clear on what evangelism is and actually do it.

A SHIFT IN OUR HOLINESS THINKING

We need to shift the way we see mission, and we need to shift the way we understand evangelism. We also must shift the way we see holiness or the life of conversion we are called to live as disciples. We must move away from a paradigm that suggests we are formed spiritually by how much we know. Instead, we must understand holiness as the process by which we are being made into the image of God, in which we were created.

Emerging generations hear or see the word "holiness," and they think of a set of rigid rules that keep us from enjoying life. As you know, an accurate understanding of holiness is not about being restrained by rigid rules; it is about freedom to live the way in which we were meant to live. The mission of God is to restore the world toward its intended wholeness. Evangelism invites people into becoming disciples who seek to live whole, garden-like lives. Holiness, then, is the process by which we are restored to our soul in its primitive health—pure and intended to will one thing: wholeness. Holiness is not a stationary life; it is a dynamic life that is about increasing the health of our created soul. Holiness is about increasing the frequency and duration of the holy moments in our life. Holiness is living in such a way that creates more and more distance between the screwups in our life. Holiness, in the end, is pure love—

mutual love between God and mankind, and mankind and mankind in God's love.

We recently surveyed over five hundred Christian Millennials and asked them, "What is holiness?" Here are the results:

- 67%—not sinning;
- 13%—being religious;
- 11%—becoming like Jesus;
- 9%—not really sure.

As you can see, to 67% of the five hundred-plus Christian Millennials we asked, holiness has nothing to do with bringing forth God's kingdom reign or making the world whole; it only has to do with not sinning. I realize that holiness is increasing the frequency and duration of the holy moments in our lives, so yes—it does have to do with not sinning. However, why are we in pursuit of a sinless or life of less sin anyway—for the sake of personal piety? No, of course not. We are in pursuit of holiness to create garden-like environments where people can experience God's power, peace, provision, and presence, and toward a whole world as it was created to be.

So much of creating a proper concept of holiness has to do not only with how we define it on paper, but with how we define it with our words and actions. We asked the same group of people referenced above (five hundred Christian Millennials) if they thought people really wanted to change their lives to become more holy. Nearly 50% said no; about 30% said maybe; 15% said yes; and 5% said not sure. This means we have a credibility issue. We say we want to be people of holiness, but our words don't back it up. Words are hollow until we give them meaning with our lives. Even Millennials who are Christians think (at least 50% of them we surveyed) that people really aren't all that interested in changing the way they live. Clearly, even if they did think people were willing to change their lives to become holy people, according to the stats above, 67% of them wouldn't even know why.

We must rethink the reason we are striving for holiness and, at the same time, change the way we define holiness—on paper and with our lives. We must see holiness as:

1. **The way to a garden-like life.** As I have already mentioned, holiness should not be understood first and foremost as the absence of sin. Rather, it should be sin as a means to creating, sustaining, and experiencing a world that resembles the garden of Eden, the garden of Jesus' tomb, and the garden of the new city, in which the power, peace, provision, and presence of God prevails. We do not pursue holiness for personal piety; we pursue holiness to honor God and participate with God to restore the world toward its intended wholeness.

2. **Grace winning over guilt.** If we truly believe that God is a gracious God who gifts the freedom of a new life through the birth, life, death, resurrection, and ascension of Jesus, then we must live knowing that grace is bigger than guilt—or that life has already defeated death. Yes, we should feel the weight of our words and actions that miss God's intended mark for our life, but we should never focus or make others focus on guilt. Jesus died so that we don't have to feel the shame and blame any longer. Sitting in guilt means that we are stripping God's glory away from God. When guilt wins, God looks small. When grace wins, God look big.

3. **Awaken to the Spirit.** Every person has been gifted the breath of God. God is the source of life, and we received life because God breathed God's Spirit into us. Christians are people with Christ living within us. Christ living within us means that the Holy Spirit has been awakened within us, and we now receive the gifts Jesus promised, like comfort, counsel, guidance, teaching, conviction, and so forth. Christians need to close the credibility gap that emerging generations see between what we say we want and what we actually will allow God to change in us. Christian, you have the Holy Spirit, so live like it. Live with confidence knowing that the Holy Spirit is present, giving you everything you need to live a holy life marked by love—humility, hope, and wholeness.

4. **Confession is freedom.** Admitting to God our shortcomings or places in our life where we miss the mark awakens forgiveness. Forgiveness allows for freedom. When we tell God the truth and we tell others the truth, we open feelings of liberty we never even knew we had. Freedom from sin is not that you live a sinless life, necessarily. Freedom from sin is a life in which sin doesn't rule over you. Let freedom reign, and move toward repentance.

5. **Repentance is worship.** When we repent, that is, change our life through our thoughts, attitudes, and behavior, we worship God. Holiness is the radiance of God's glory. Our mind is renewed when our heart is changed. When our heart is changed or transformed spiritually, we reflect glory to God, and this is holiness. When we mourn our sin and make a resolution to allow God to change our character, we live more fully into the life God intended for us. God is worshipped and praised when we repent.

6. **Prayer is the path.** Not really all that much to say here except to acknowledge that when we pray, we put ourselves in a posture of need and remembrance. We remind ourselves that God is the granter of grace and that we need God's grace to sustain our daily walk toward wholeness. Not to mention, when we pray as a means toward holiness, we slow down and allow for reflection, meditation, and solitude to center us or align us with God's mission for the world.

7. **Living for a community, not for yourself.** I used to think that my sin was just mine, and it didn't impact others. That notion couldn't be further from the truth. If we are going to help people—emerging generations in particular—see holiness in a new light, we must change the way we think of missing the mark. Missing the mark is sin, and sin is darkness and death. The mission of God is to restore the world toward its intended wholeness—all of creation. To miss the mark God has set for us, therefore, is to feed into the brokenness not the wholeness. When we neglect God's intended way for our lives, we impact all those around us. Sin is bigger than the "stuff" that we do; it is also the work in the world that we leave untouched like poverty, destruction, racism, and so forth. Bottom line: God's mark is wholeness, and anything we do or don't do that doesn't move us closer to heaven on earth is missing the mark.

Holiness is a key ingredient to bringing about garden-like settings in which we are allowing people to experience the transcendence of God. In order for us to capture the imagination of emerging generations, we must rethink the way we teach about holiness. This rethinking must create a new paradigm that continues to involve the importance of holiness, but gives way to a life of greater purpose and meaning, common good, and possibility of a world made whole.

A SHIFT IN OUR LEADERSHIP THINKING

In order to move toward an asset-based community discipleship model as I have outlined previously in this chapter, we must shift our thinking on mission, evangelism, holiness, and leadership. As we move toward a model that gets out of our church, opens up our lives, and commits to reach the people with whom we have either direct or indirect influence, we'll need to deploy a leadership structure that changes to accommodate this new thinking. We must (1) move away from a one-size-fits-all model, (2) shift the power from the platform to the people, (3) acknowledge culture as it is and stop its mighty current, and (4) stop trying to be perfect leaders.

One-size-fits-all model of leadership isn't helpful. As leaders, we must be able to navigate the changing landscape of our world, the individual makeup of the people we lead, and our own evolving style of leading. I believe leadership is an activity and anyone can do it. I also believe, however, that our activity of leadership cannot be the same for each situation and for each person we lead. We must lead with more of a one-size-fits-one mentality, where we take the time to address the specific needs of the people we lead and the unique set of circumstances in which we lead. In my twenty or more years of leading people in church, business, nonprofits, and military settings, I have learned that my leadership style is nothing more than what I would call adaptive, and by that I mean useful in any and all types of situations.

The platform carries certain power or influence with it. Along with the power is also a weight or a burden that is ripe with responsibility. In an asset-based community discipleship model where we are proclaiming, preforming, and maintaining presence with the gospel, we need to shift the power from the platform to the pew, or to the people. This doesn't mean we shirk the responsibility and avoid the burden, giving it to someone else. Rather, shifting the power entails empowering others to lead, even at the risk of inefficiency, failure, or a divergent path forward. Shifting the power enables communities to see themselves as key players in the change or vision and allows the entirety of the group or groups of people we lead to lead with their own set of assets, not our set transferred upon them. Sustainable leadership is possible when we give the people around us the chance to engage and contribute in meaningful ways.

We need to shift away from thinking we can change culture and instead embrace it, knowing that our efforts might be more effective when we help people experience a sudden shift or jolt. As I mentioned in the introduction, I spent a lot of time at my grandfather's property during the summer months. At the east end of his acreage, there was a creek. This creek (pronounced "crick" in much of the northeast part of the US) was usually very swift. My brothers and I would try to dam up the creek to make a wading pool. We would spend hours placing large rocks on one another the width of the creek and do our best to dam it up. At times, we were able to create a pool up to our waists. We'd come back a day or so later and the force of the current would have displaced the rocks, and we'd have to build the dam over again. It was a never-ending encounter. We loved it and hated it all at the same time. Culture is like this—it is moving swiftly in a particular direction. The sheer force of the water flow was unstoppable. We could make a dent in the water, so to speak, every once in a while, but we were never able to build a complete dam. After a while, instead of building dams, we built boats and raced them. It is time that we use culture to our advantage, shift our thinking that we must avoid it, and make the most out of what we are designed to do.

Recently I was talking with my son whose name is Drew. I asked him about stepping up at church and being a leader. I said, "Drew, I bet if you were more vocal in our confirmation class and if you engaged consistently, the others would follow. I think it is time for you to step up your game and be a leader." His response was, "I can't be a leader; I am not perfect."

Somewhere along the line we have created this fiction that leaders are perfect, or at the very least, have their lives all sorted out and together. The truth of it, however, is that like those around us, our life is a mess in areas too. We need help too. We need to realize that by projecting a false notion that our lives are in order gives the impression that to be a leader, you have to have it all together. My son is like so many other young adults I talk to about leadership. They don't want to lead because they know, very authentically I might add, that their life is in need of improvement. To get the most out of the assets people have, we must stop pretending that we have it all together and be more willing to share our failures and shortcomings in order that we might welcome new leaders and invest in them to make disciples in our community.

We must reimagine the way we think of and practice leadership and, in doing so, develop a leadership paradigm in our churches that:

1. **Anticipates and adapts to the constant change.** Leaders have to be willing to try new methods in order to meet the shifting landscape. From generational differences to new technologies to cultural challenges—leaders must be ready to anticipate change and adapt to meet the demands of that change. Leadership ingenuity is as needed as ever before.

2. **Discovers and maximizes the set of assets of the people around us.** People can lead, so let them do it. The people who comprise our churches, for the most part, are fully capable of leading. Many of them lead in various ways in their professional life and are adept at leading in most settings. Granted, some may share a different value system and have a different process for making decisions, and leaders who can lead a one-sits-fits-one type of context welcome the differences in others. Many church leaders that I meet are control freaks. They need to be less so and allow others to have some control.

3. **Embraces the set of cultural uniqueness in our community.** As we've mentioned in several places throughout this book, every community is different. My church has four campuses. Each of the campuses is in a different setting in our metro area. This means that the challenges facing these churches, and quite possibly the solutions needed to address them, are likely going to be different. Exegete the culture, determine the unique challenges, and address them accordingly. It is also important that when we exegete the culture to determine the context, we also discover and claim the opportunities for success as well as the challenges. So many leaders I meet are unable to celebrate the strengths of the community and the potential places where impact can ignite the fire within the community because they are so diligent to only magnify the challenges. Today's great leaders can find both the challenges and the opportunities, and work toward the necessary solutions and the assets to exploit.

4. **Increases the authenticity quotient and stops trying to create the sense that we are better or more together than we really are.** Like many of you, I have followed many different types of leaders over my twenty-plus years of ministry. The leaders who have made the most impact on my life are the leaders who have been vulnerable and

genuine. Leaders who have taken the time to be present with me—sharing their weaknesses, shortcomings, insecurities, and fears—are the leaders I remember most. The leaders who are willing to appropriately share with their followers are the leaders who can help young emerging leaders make sense of the weaknesses, shortcomings, insecurities, and fears that they deal with, and then know how to navigate through them as they can often paralyze young leaders. The kinds of leaders that are most inspiring and charismatic leaders to me are the ones who can share openly about their growth areas in life.

5. **Engages the whole community in leadership, not just the people we like or want to be around.** There is a phrase that I am sure you've heard once or twice in your life that goes something like, "Life is short. I only want to work with people I like." I understand that statement, and I get the intent behind it. However, to me, that is one of the most arrogant and ill-considered statements any leader can make. Leaders who will effectively lead churches toward an asset-based community discipleship model will be leaders who can find the assets of everyone in the congregation and leverage those assets to more effectively and faithfully participate in God's mission to restore the world toward its intended wholeness. The most effective leaders I have ever seen have the skills and abilities to maximize their leadership capacity in others around them, even if they are difficult people to be around. Personalities clash, and some people are just plain hard to be around. Chances are we've all been that person a time or two.

We've covered a lot of ground in this chapter, as we discussed the four primary paradigm shifts that must be made in order to become a church that best reaches and engages Millennials and Generation Z.

In the next chapter, we will discuss a detailed model of how a church can take the concept of asset-based community discipleship and deploy it in a practical, effective, and compelling way.

CHAPTER 6

A MODEL FOR MINISTRY ACROSS GENERATIONS

Emerging generations are not the only people who need to be reached and engaged with the gospel. Clearly, this post-Christian world in which we live is filled with spiritual but not religious people of all generations and mindsets. I believe the gospel such as revealed through the garden-like life God intended for us in which people can experience transcendence by experiencing God's power, peace, provision, and presence.

The garden resonates with all people. The way in which we proclaim, perform, and make present the gospel to each person we come in contact with may be different. In the end, however, the gospel story penetrates the heart, stimulates the mind, and activates the hands and feet of all who believe.

While I contend that we are in a one-size-fits-one culture and that discipleship is not an exercise in assembly-line production, I think it is incredibly important that we have a working or practical theology of discipleship. Out of a practical theology of discipleship, we develop pathways for people to experience the transformational life in ways pertinent directly to them.

I joined the staff of my church five years ago. Since coming on staff, I have led the charge on developing a theological framework that is built on the four pillars of what I referred to in an earlier chapter as asset-based community discipleship—mission, evangelism, holiness, and leadership.

While we do not necessarily use the term *asset-based community discipleship* on a regular basis, we do talk almost daily about what a narrative-missional theological framework looks like and how we can disciple people across generations. The following is the framework that we use to strategically disciple people and equip them with the tools to make disciples. This framework also keeps us accountable to a narrative-missional, whole-gospel commitment, and at the same time helps us evaluate our intentions, plans, and results.

I'll confess that sometimes when I teach this theological framework, I get significant pushback. The pushback comes in two main areas. First, some people hear me teach on this and think that it is too corporate and not organic enough or relational enough. Second, some people hear me teach on this and think that it is too simple—that it doesn't allow discipleship to be messy and real. Some people think that this framework or what we call our discipleship pyramid, simply because of its shape, is too neat, tidy, and organized.

Before I explain the pyramid and then later make some specific statements about how this can work with Millennials and Generation Z, I'd like to address the two main areas of pushback that I frequently receive when I present the pyramid as a way in which to develop people.

First of all, discipleship is all about relationships—incarnational relationships. Effective discipleship involves a relationship in three ways: relationship between disciple-maker and God, the person being discipled and God, and the disciple and disciple-maker. Discipleship without organic relationships is impossible, especially since disciple-making happens best one-on-one or in small communities.

Regarding the second critique, relationships are inherently messy. People will make you mad. People will let you down. People will be untruthful with you. People will hide things from you. People will have things happen to them that are painful and just plain tough to deal with . . . and all of those things are true for you as well. Nothing about being in relationships is neat, tidy, and packaged with a bow.

The discipleship pyramid described as follows cannot be effective in an assembly-line production kind of way. The programs associated with each of the five dimensions of the pyramid in our church or in any church are just portals for relationship. We bring people together for classes, groups, events, and retreats, not because any of those things are an end to themselves, but because they are ways in which to connect with people for the purpose of establishing relationships in which disciples are being made and mentored.

The discipleship pyramid built upon the four pillars of mission, evangelism, holiness, and leadership development, consists of five dimensions of ongoing conversion. The five dimensions of ongoing conversion are (1) exploring God, (2) encountering God, (3) engaging God's story and people, (4) expressing God's mission, and (5) embodying God's mission.

DIMENSION 1: EXPLORING GOD

This dimension of the discipleship pyramid is the beginning of the conversion experience. In this dimension, people are given the opportunity to explore God. This exploration dimension could be experienced through worship services, missions, or service work; outreach events, personal invitations, or special programs that allow interested and curious people to investigate the claims of gospel. For some, this dimension is a brand-new experience, and for others this dimension is a return to a previous experience in which they sought to better understand the claims of the gospel.

DIMENSION 2: ENCOUNTERING GOD

People encounter God in many ways, such as through all of the opportunities listed in the first dimension, especially worship services and personal invitations. Most churches are very good when it comes to programming for this mission because it typically involves the weekend worship services. Many churches spend most of their time focusing on the weekend worship services and, as a result, churches can provide an excellent way to encounter God.

I believe, however, that along with the importance of the focused attention given to worship services, it is what transpires around the worship services that are most important. Hospitality is likely the most important aspect of providing a place for people to encounter God in your church campus. If people do not feel welcome personally and do not sense an overall spirit of openness and generosity, they will probably not stay.

DIMENSION 3: ENGAGING GOD'S STORY AND PEOPLE

In this dimension of the conversion process, people are making sense of the Bible as a guide for life (missionally speaking, not as a rulebook) and beginning to understand the importance of connecting with one another in communities or micro-congregations. It is at this phase of the pyramid that people recognize how critical it is to be in a community in which together, the four pillars of mission, evangelism, holiness, and leadership development are the foundation for a life made whole.

I presently serve at a very large church. Many of the people whom I speak to tell me how hard it is to get connected to a group where they can learn, find fellowship, feel cared for, challenge each other to live holy lives, and serve others. This as we see in the early church (Acts 2:42-47) is the essence of what it looks like to be in a biblical and missional community. The truth of it, however, is that it is difficult to find a group like this in a medium or small church too. This is simply because community is hard, and it is much easier to remain disengaged and "practice the faith" in isolation.

Churches that desire to move toward an asset-based community discipleship model must prioritize the importance of connecting people into a group where individuals can flourish in their faith and bring their faith into the community for all to thrive.

DIMENSION 4: EXPRESSING GOD'S MISSION

As a person continues to explore God, encounter God, and engage in God's story and people, the conversion process (ultimate goal: wholeness!) begins to create a passion and priority for leading and serving both inside and outside the walls of the church. At this point in the growth process, people across generations begin to discover their assets, such as spiritual gifts, interests, passions, social causes, and deploy their assets for the good of the community.

In this dimension, people find a way to begin discipling others and also places to serve. Some feel compelled to serve as an usher or greeter. Others feel compelled to teach a Sunday school class or lead a confirmation group. Still others choose to go on mission trips or launch a new initiative altogether, like a lunchtime Bible study in their office, and so forth. It is at this point in the conversion process that people can no longer stand by. In order to grow in their faith, they have to find a place to lead and serve.

DIMENSION 5: EMBODYING GOD'S MISSION

The goal of this Christian life is Christ living in us. Or said differently, the goal of this Christian is to embody the person and work of Jesus. When someone says the goal of the Christian life is to "live like Jesus," that is true. To live like Jesus, however, is to live into the image in which we have been created or to live as God intended for us to live—a garden-like life that is marked first and foremost by love.

We are called to be holy people. In one sense, we are already holy as we are sanctified or set apart. In another sense, we are called to a life of holiness or of conversion toward wholeness, which is a total love for God and others.

Embodying the person and work of Jesus is to live missionally. It is to live for the sake of the world. Our job as leaders in the church is to call and equip all people, regardless of generation or mindset, to participate with God in God's mission to restore the world toward its intended wholeness. When a person's life of conversion leads them to embody the person and work of Jesus, it means that they are representing God with their whole life. Christians cannot escape this reality. As you know, it is not enough to go to church; we must be the church—the agency that God is empowering through the presence and ministry of the Holy Spirit to be ambassadors of reconciliation or wholeness.

As you can see, when a person grows through the conversion process from exploration to embodiment, they move toward the symbol they were created to be in God's design, the garden of Eden. The job of pastors, lay-staff ministers, and volunteers is to faithfully help people grow in their faith and experience ongoing transformation.

I present this discipleship pyramid for two reasons. First, I want to give those of you who do not have a stated theology of discipleship to use the one that I have created for your church to help people into a life of conversion. Second, I want to help us remember that there are multiple generations in the church today, not just Millennials and Generation Z. While I believe that we need to focus a great deal of our attention toward reaching and engaging Millennials and Generation Z, we cannot do this at the expense of other generations.

In fact, I believe that one of the best ways to reach Millennials and Generation Z is to engage and equip the parents and grandparents of your church to reach their own children and grandchildren. Over the last year, we have had several successful attempts at starting new groups of Millennials because their parents were intentional about inviting them to church and into a life of following Jesus.

There is nothing for sure about the discipleship pyramid we employ at our church to reach and engage people to help them become deeply committed Christians. While the pyramid isn't a guaranteed way to disciple people, it is just that, a way. We are always changing the way in which we attempt to best help people grow. Where we are taking them, however, never changes. We are taking people on a pilgrimage toward a life of faithful participation on the mission of God and readying them to lead others into the process.

WHAT THE CONVERSION PROCESS LOOKS LIKE FOR SOME PEOPLE

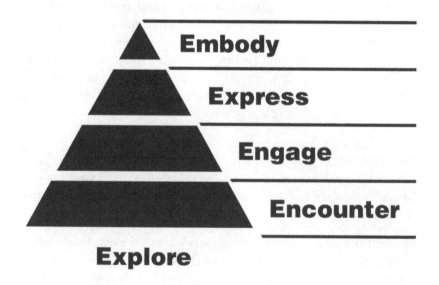

Embody

Express

Engage

Encounter

Explore

The process, as I have already mentioned, is not a one-size-fits-all model. It is a model that requires specific attention to the uniqueness of people, a one-size-fits-one model that requires a commitment to mission, evangelism, holiness, and leadership. The programs we employ in our church to leverage as portals of relationship will look different for several reasons. First, context is everything. Since our cultural contexts are different, the pathway we use to help people grow in their faith will also be different.

Second, we are all different leaders. We are driven by different passions, have interests in different matters, are designed with different gifts, and use our influence to lead others differently. This means that our programs or pathways will look and function differently.

Finally, our churches are different sizes and require a different set of logistics to operate effectively. It is important, however, that regardless of the size of your church, you have a context and leader-specific theology of discipleship that helps people become more deeply committed Christians.

FIVE KEY CONSIDERATIONS FOR THE DISCIPLESHIP PYRAMID IN ORDER TO BE EFFECTIVE WITH EMERGING GENERATIONS[58]

The emphasis for this book is to help churches reach and engage emerging generations. While it is critical to keep in mind that the church is made up of multiple generations, all who deserve to be reached and engaged, it is also critical that we provide a way to reach younger people who are living in this post-Christian world.

We long to see our churches and communities filled with young people who are compelled by the gospel story and who choose to faithfully live out the virtues of Jesus. We long for our churches to be filled not for our own egos and practical realities like paying bills and building maintenance, but so the world might be made whole through the faithful commitment participating with God's mission to restore the world toward its intended wholeness.

For us to connect with emerging generations in an asset-based community discipleship framework and to help them grow in their faith, our discipleship strategies must include several considerations. As each generation is different, our specific attempts to reach and engage them

---

58. http://www.ministrymatters.com/all/entry/6040/what-millennials-crave-and-how-the-church-can-relate

must keep in mind their uniqueness as we plan and execute that plan. Following are five considerations to keep in mind when inviting emerging generations to explore God, encounter God, engage God's story and people, express God's mission, and embody the person and work of Jesus.

CONSIDERATION #1: ENGAGEMENT OVER INTERRUPTION

Emerging generations don't want to be interrupted; they want to be engaged in the midst of their already existing life. Emerging generations want frictionless opportunities to engage faith. For many of us, the mobile devices we carry are solely about productivity and efficiency first. We love the technology that we carry in our pockets, but it is typically first and foremost for making life easier, specifically our work life. Emerging generations also want this productivity and efficiency. However, more important than a productive life is a connected life—a life in which you can be present with someone and be hundreds of miles away. Churches must find ways to engage emerging generations in ways that do not interrupt their lives but cooperate with them.

CONSIDERATION #2: INTERACTION OVER REACTION

Emerging generations crave experiences. This means that as churches desiring to connect with them, we are not just giving them a list of to-dos to carry out on their own time. Instead, we must find ways to interact with Millennials in shared experiences that allow for faith to be practiced in community, not just talked about in isolation. The more the experience is interactive or collaborative, the greater the interest level. The interest in emerging generations to practice faithful living is directly proportionate to the collaboration of the experiences you are creating to engage them.

CONSIDERATION #3: EMPOWERED PARTICIPANTS OVER ATTENDANCE

Emerging generations want to be empowered. They want to know that what they are being asked to do is contributing to something bigger than themselves. While some people, from any and every generation, want to just sit back and be a consumer, most people (and Millennials and Generation Z are no different) want to make a difference. Part of empowering emerging generations is mentoring them, investing in their development (personally and professionally), and giving them a job to do.

Emerging generations want to lead and be a part of the whole. To reach and engage Millennials and Generation Z, your church will need to find ways—multiple, life-giving ways—to empower them to contribute to the church and community in meaningful, challenging ways.

CONSIDERATION #4: PERSONAL GESTURES OVER BIG PROMISES

We make a lot of promises on God's behalf about what God wants to do in this world. We shout it from the platform each weekend with great passion and determination. Our churches are filled with people who present God through big promises, such as "God loves you and has a plan for your life," "God will never leave you," "God loves you so much," and so forth. Then, when people need those promises to be fulfilled the most, they are left trying to make sense as to why they have to figure things out on their own. Like all people, emerging generations want to see people's personal gestures back up the big promises they hear. In the words of a young adult who recently came into my office to see me, "Everyone talks about how God is always with me, and then this crap happens and I feel all alone. In fact, I have never felt more alone. Everyone knows what happened to me, and not one person has asked me about it." The way God is present with people is through the church being the church. Big promises need to give way to genuine, consistent, personal gestures that prove God is who we say God is.

CONSIDERATION #5: PARTNERS OVER MEMBERS

For emerging generations, there is much more significance in being viewed as driving the bus, so to speak, than merely on it for a ride from here to there. People want to participate in what they value. Churches must create a value proposition that goes beyond "Come to church," and instead invites people to "Be the church." The value of belonging to something is not enough. Emerging generations are bored by and find no lasting value in simply being along for the ride. Community is important to emerging generations, yes. Community with a cause is compelling and has a higher value. The greater our value proposition or call to be more than a member, the greater the opportunity we have to engage emerging generations. From very early in our lives, we all felt the difference between memberships in the club which was way cool, to being in leadership of the club which was way cooler. Emerging generations want to be partners and leaders and co-contributors now, not when you are ready to hand off your leadership role because you are tired or burned out.

We need a strategic plan and process to reach and engage emerging generations. This plan and process needs to be bigger than any one particular mindset, and engage all the people in the church. Use the model previously listed, the discipleship pyramid, as the basis for your plan and process. Contextualize the pyramid to fit your church and leadership best, and start developing the kinds of people who use their assets to disciple others for the sake of the world.

CHAPTER 7

FINAL THOUGHTS AND GROUP-DISCUSSION QUESTIONS

We live in a post-Christian context. Millennials and Gen Z are living in a day we can no longer assume is guided by Christian values. For some leaders, this is troubling and it causes them a great deal of angst as they wonder who will fill their churches decades from now. For other leaders like me, there is still a great hope that the gospel, when proclaimed, performed, and made humbly present in compelling ways, will resonate. Yes, the times are challenging, but the kingdom of God is never in trouble.

Millennials and Gen Z, like generations gone before them, seek purpose and meaning, common good for all, and possess great optimism for the possibility of a better world. This is why the gospel resonates with emerging generations. The gospel provides the purpose and meaning, results in the common good, and is certainly full of adventure and possibility.

The gardens in the Bible, namely the garden of Eden, the garden of Jesus' tomb, and the garden of the new city, provide the necessary environment in which to re-create in order that emerging generations can see what the world was intended to be like. The gardens are filled with God's power, peace, provision, and presence, and offer the hope of all things made new.

These garden-like environments that we make real in our daily lives emit signals of transcendence. These signals of transcendence help emerging generations to see something in the gospel story and Kingdom ethics that is bigger than them. The signals of transcendence that we share with emerging generations provide a sense of awe, shalom, life, and intimacy, and reveal the supernatural—the extraordinary. This is the key in reaching emerging generations to help them experience the astonishing and unexpected, and ask questions like, *Who are you?* and *Where are you from?*

Our churches need a commitment to new paradigms that change the way we view the discipleship process. We need to construct a way forward to reach and engage emerging generations that highlights the transcendent moments in life, and at the same time closes the believability gap that exists between what we say and how we live. Mission, evangelism, holiness, and leadership are four pillars of asset-based community discipleship that take discipleship into the community and allow for a shared experience within our church walls. For churches to successfully reach and engage emerging generations, we must empower our congregations to live garden-like lives that prove the gospel of the Kingdom to be real.

As our churches construct new ways of building discipleship models on the four pillars of mission, evangelism, holiness, and leadership, we must construct a model that reaches across all generations and calls for a churchwide equipping-and-sending model that re-creates the garden's key attributes and faithfully participates in God's mission to restore the world toward its intended wholeness.

Above all, churches and leaders, we need hope. Jesus Christ came to die for us, but also to show us how to live. Jesus, in his life, death, burial, resurrection, and ascension, gave us new life—a life marked by hope, victory, and eternality. For our churches to reach emerging generations, we must patiently yet profoundly live into this hope.

QUESTIONS FOR GROUP DISCUSSION

Chapter 1

- In your own words, what does it mean that we are living in a post-Christian world?

- Why do you think it is so hard for some leaders to change and adapt to meet the needs of the emerging generations?

- Do you agree with the author's definition of the gospel on page 14? What is missing? What would you add to the author's definition?

- Does the gospel change? Why or why not?

- The author shares several statistics about Millennials. Did any of these statistics surprise you? Which ones were surprises?

- The author gives seven core values and behaviors of Millennials. In what ways have you personally experienced these to be true?

- The author shares several statistics about Generation Z. Did any of these statistics surprise you? Which ones were surprises?

- The author gives seven core values and behaviors of Generation Z. In what ways have you personally experienced these to be true?

- Have you found your purpose in life? What is it?

- Do you agree with the author that within the framework of the gospel, purpose and meaning, common good, and possibility exist? Why or why not?

Chapter 2

- The author gives five descriptions of the gospel on pages 32–33. Do you agree with these descriptions? Yes or no? Why or why not?

- On pages 35–36, the author provides several descriptions of the kingdom of God. Do you agree with these descriptions? Why or why not? What would you add or describe differently?

- The author uses a story from his past to describe how the gospel will translate to and capture the imagination of emerging generations. In what ways do you think you can personally make them a reality in your everyday relationships?

Chapter 3

- In what ways do gardens help us see the way God intended for the world to be?

- Have you ever spent time in a garden? Describe those experiences. How did they make you feel?

- What do we know about the garden of Eden?

- What do we know about the garden of Jesus' tomb?

- What do we know about the garden of the new city?

- The author provides four key factors that can be found within each of the gardens—power, peace, provision, and presence. In what ways would you describe these four factors?

- What reasons can you give for these four factors being essential? In other words, why do these four P words matter?

- The author provides practical ways to cultivate garden-like environments on pages 58–60. What are some other ways you can think of that would cultivate garden-like environments?

Chapter 4

- According to the author, what is the key to reaching and engaging emerging generations? Do you agree? Why or why not?

- How would you describe the narrative of relevance? What are some stories you have of churches trying too hard to be relevant? What are some stories you have in which churches have been successful with their relevance?

- How would you describe the narrative of counterculture? What are some stories you have of churches trying too hard to be countercultural? What are some stories you have in which churches have been successful with their commitment to being countercultural?

- Describe what signals (or signs) of transcendence are. What signals have you experienced in your life?

- The author provides four biblical narratives that reveal moments of transcendence, all of which include a question, such as, *Who are you?* What other narratives can you think of in Scripture that provide a window into a transcendent experience?

- What other kinds of questions have you personally encountered that people ask in amazement and that reveal a transcendent experience?

- The author provided ten key traits we can practice to help people experience the transcendent. Do you agree or disagree with any of them? What would you add to the author's list?

Chapter 5

- According to the author, what is asset-based community discipleship?

- What does it mean to follow Jesus?

- What is the goal of discipleship?

- The author lists four paradigm shifts needed to develop an asset-based community discipleship model. Do you agree with the four? Why or why not?

- What does mission mean in an asset-based community discipleship model?

- Do you agree that a narrative theological framework is necessary to understand mission? Why or why not?

- What is evangelism in an asset-based community discipleship model?

- Describe holiness in an asset-based community discipleship model.

- In what ways must our leadership paradigm shift?

Chapter 6

- Describe your personal theology of discipleship.

- In your own words, what do you think it means to be made in the image of God? Yes or no, is this the pursuit of the Christian life?

- Do you feel it critical to have a discipleship model that transcends generations? Why or why not?

- How do you feel about the discipleship pyramid the author suggests?

- The author provides five considerations when reaching emerging generations with a model of discipleship. Do you agree or disagree with them? What would you add to the list?

- Does your church have a strategic plan for discipling people? If so, describe it. If not, why do you think that is?

- Why is contextualization so important to the discipleship process?

NOTES

By providing relevant and affordable products and resources, real-time consulting, practical on-site, regional based training and ongoing research, Burlap helps churches of all sizes revitalize their congregations.

Burlap offers hope-based solutions to reach millennials and generation Z throughout the entire scope of its work throughout North America. We can help your church navigate the changing cultural landscape by discovering already-existing assets within your church and community to create new stories of hope and renewal.

burlap

www.ThinkBurlap.com

CPSIA information can be obtained
at www.ICGtesting.com
Printed in the USA
LVHW05s1600270718
585151LV00010B/654/P